I Say...
So I Am

A Proclamation
of **Royalty**

For Tweens & Teens

Mya C. Huff

Presented To:

_____
_____

From:

_____
_____

Occasion:

_____
_____

Special Note:

_____
_____
_____
_____
_____

I Say…So I Am: A Proclamation of Royalty
For Tweens and Teens

ISBN 978-0-9906520-2-1
eISBN 978-0-9906520-3-8

Copyright © 2011, 2015 by Mya Huff
www.myahuff.org

All rights reserved. No portion of this book may be reproduced in any form whatsoever, without the written permission of the copyright owner.

Unless otherwise noted, all Scripture quotations are from the NIV Worship Bible, The New International Version. Copyright 2000 by the Corinthian Group, Inc. All rights reserved.

Scripture quotations marked KJV are from The Holy Bible, King James Version Large Print Thinline Edition. Copyright 2009 by Zondervan. All rights reserved.

To order copies in bulk please contact: *info@MyaHuff.org*.

Due to the formatting of this book there may be certain portions that are not available in the eBook version. We ask eBook readers to keep a notebook or journal to record their daily progress and thoughts during this journey. God Bless

PRINTED IN THE UNITED STATES OF AMERICA

DEDICATION

This book is dedicated to my nephews, Micah and Mehki. The concept started with a poster of confessions I created for you guys to say daily. You have been a light and joy in my life. I know that God is going to do mighty things through both of you. Remember that you are princes—simply because you belong to God.

TABLE OF CONTENTS

Preface

Explanation of Daily Sections

DAY 1: Exercising Power	1
DAY 2: The God Encounter	9
DAY 3: God's Love	16
DAY 4: Better Than Sacrifice	23
DAY 5: Leadership	30
DAY 6: Understanding	36
DAY 7: Potential	44
DAY 8: My Identity	51
God's Prince	52
God's Princess	58
DAY 9: God I Agree	65
DAY 10: Favor	72
DAY 11: Stand	77
DAY 12: Give Thanks	82
DAY 13: Friends	88

DAY 14: Humility   95

DAY 15: Designed to Rule   100

DAY 16: Forgiveness   106

DAY 17: I'm Better   113

DAY 18: Keep Going!   119

DAY 19: Truthful   126

DAY 20: Happiness   131

DAY 21: Complete   137

DAY 22: Diligence   142

DAY 23: More Than Enough   148

DAY 24: Healing   154

DAY 25: Creative Power   160

DAY 26: Carrier of Glory   167

DAY 27: Love   173

DAY 28: Seeds   180

DAY 29: Salvation   186

DAY 30: Holy Spirit   191

DAY 31: Freedom   195

DAY 32: Safe In His Arms	200
DAY 33: Trust God	207
DAY 34: Living Flame	213
DAY 35: Zeal	219
DAY 36: Family and Unity	224
DAY 37: Optimistic	231
DAY 38: Well Done	236
DAY 39: Something New	241
DAY 40: And It Was So	247
Create Your Own Confessions	253
School Day Ready!	255
List of Daily Confessions	256
Notes	

Preface

Prayer through Christ Jesus is how we connect with the realms of God. We must reach into the heavenly realm every day. Even though we presently exist in this world. The laws of heaven govern the earth and every other dimension beyond this world. We have the power to affect what takes place in the spirit realm. As humans, we should tap into the spirit realm only through Christ Jesus and His blood. The blood of Jesus is a rite of passage for humanity to come into the presence of God.

When Jesus Christ died, the Bible says the veil was torn in two. *(Matthew 27:50-51)* Christ Jesus is the mediator between God and man. We are to come boldly before the throne of grace. You are *always* welcomed in God's presence.

1 Timothy 2:4-5 This is good, and pleases God our Savior, who wants all men to be saved and to come to a knowledge of the truth. For there is one God and one mediator between God and men, the man Christ Jesus, who gave himself as a ransom for all men....(NIV)

Hebrews 4:16 Let us then approach the throne of grace with confidence, so that we may receive mercy and find grace to help us in our time of need (NIV).

Throughout this book you will call forth things from the heavenly realm to be made manifest in the earthly realm. You will also learn to put into practice what you are confessing over yourself. Sometimes people make the mistake of thinking that asking is enough. The truth is you have to give effort and position yourself to receive what you are asking God for. In this book, you will operate in power every single day, and that will happen through the Word of God. From now on, you will confess blessings over your life. You will come into agreement with who God says you are. You will shift things in the spirit realm, aligning them with God's divine will and plan for your life.

The enemy knows he has no power to cast any spell over a believer in Christ Jesus. The enemy depends on believers' casting spells and snares over themselves through negative confessions and poor decisions. A spell is anything that encourages or causes behavior that is contrary to who God says you are to be. It manipulates your way of thinking and your perception in an ungodly way. Take inventory of the music you listen to, the TV shows you watch, and the conversations you have. Is it possible that you have confessed something over yourself or welcomed something into your spirit or mind that is contrary to God?

In part, this is the way *The American Heritage Dictionary* defines the following words:

- Spell: 1a. A word or formula believed to have magic power. b. A bewitched state; trance. 2. Allure; fascination[1]

- Snare: 1. A trap 2. Something that entangles[2]

- Stronghold: A fortress[3]

Do you have fascination with something that God has set Himself against? Has the enemy tried to build a fortress of deception around you to keep you entangled? Guess what? God can break every spell and stronghold the enemy has tried to use to hinder your life. Through Christ Jesus and through His blood you will be free. You are going to take your power back! Through the power of God, the negative things will be undone. Are you ready? To fight! To conquer! To win!

Explanation of Daily Sections

This book will change your life! I want you to know there is no rush. We are going to take this journey one confession, one prayer, and one day at a time. This is your journey. The day's tasks are outlined below for your viewing. These daily sections will vary in size, and that is by design.

Today's Confession:
You will be given one confession to read aloud daily. This will get you in the habit of saying positive things over yourself. Doing so will shape your future in a positive way. Most of all, it will help you to come into agreement with what God has said about you.

What It Means To Be and What Is:
This section will define the words contained within your confession. The goal here is to help you have a clear understanding of what you are saying over yourself. Not every day's reading will contain this particular section, so if there are any words in your daily confession that you do not understand, please look them up. Doing so will increase transparency and understanding.

Bread for the Soul:
This section will contain scriptures for you to read each day. As you put more of the Word of God into yourself, you will find that His ways increasingly pour out of you. *Romans 10:17 says this: "So then faith cometh by hearing, and hearing by the word of God" (KJV).* In 2 Timothy 2:15, we are told, *"Study to shew thyself approved unto God" (KJV).* So cherish and value the Word of God. Fill yourself with it! Be a reflection of what God has written.

Today's Prayer:
This is probably the most important section of this book. You will speak aloud this particular section of your daily reading. Maybe you aren't used to praying daily or simply don't know how. This section will allow you to have at least one conversation with God per day. As human beings, it is imperative that we keep the lines of communication with Christ Jesus open. You are never too young to have a prayer life; in fact, the earlier you start, the better. God is very much looking forward to hearing from you.

Be Encouraged:
This section is simply intended to encourage you during your journey. It will give you some insight as you begin to reshape your life.

Today's Goal:
You will have one goal to accomplish each day. Such tasks will include things you can practice at home, school, and so forth.

From Your Own Perspective:
These are questions you will be able to answer in your own time. They will help you to reflect on what you have read, prayed, and confessed over yourself that day.

Daily Journal:
This section is especially for your expressions and thoughts. You can write a song, poem, or note to Jesus. You can simply write whatever you are feeling. You can talk about your goals or about where you want to be in the next forty days or so. Express what is inside of you.

Note to Reader

These declarations, prayers, and daily tasks are not meant to become obligatory religious practice in any way. They are only meant to get you in the habit of shaping your future and life in a positive way.

I Say...
So I Am

A Proclamation
of **Royalty**

For Tweens & Teens

Mya C. Huff

DAY 1: Exercising Power

Today's Confession
Read Aloud

I exercise my divine right on the earth this day to speak change into my present and future. I will decree a thing, and it will be established. I will declare a thing, and it shall come to pass.

Day 1: What It Means To Be and What Is

In part, this is the way *The American Heritage Dictionary* defines the following words:

- Divine: Superhuman; godlike.[4]

- Right: Something due to a person or governmental body by law, tradition, or nature.[5]

- Decree: An authoritative order; edict. To ordain, establish, or decide by decree.[6]

- Declare: To make known formally, officially, or authoritatively. To reveal or show. To proclaim one's support or opinion.[7]

Day 1: Bread for the Soul

Proverbs 18:21 The tongue has the power of life and death, and those who love it will eat its fruit (NIV).

Job 22:26–28 For then shalt thou have thy delight in the Almighty, and shalt lift up thy face unto God. Thou shalt make thy prayer unto him, and he shall hear thee. And thou shalt pay thou vows. Thou shalt also decree a thing, and it shall be established unto thee: and the light shall shine upon thy ways (KJV).

Matthew 16:19 I will give you the keys to kingdom of heaven: whatever you bind on earth will be bound in heaven, and whatever you loose on earth will be loosed in heaven (NIV).

Romans 4:17 ….the God who gives life to the dead and calls those things that are not as though they were (NIV).

Genesis 1:26-27 Then God said. "Let us make man in our image, in our likeness"…..So God created man in his own image, in the image of God he created him; male and female he created them (NIV)."

Day 1: Today's Prayer
Read Aloud

Christ Jesus, I thank You for the authority You have given humanity to speak into the atmosphere, giving heaven notice that we are ever in need of Your grace. Today as I pray and seek Your face, I pray that every declaration I make will be wrapped in grace as a scroll, sealed with the blood of Jesus, and brought before the throne of God. Lord, I confess that the words of my mouth will not fall to the ground but rather will be lifted to the kingdom of heaven. I pray that my words will be edifying and uplifting to myself and to those around me. Lord, help me to be mindful of what I say, and may my speech bring glory to Your Name. I speak to creation and to the realms beyond this world, commanding them to come into divine alignment with the purpose and plans that God has predestined for my life. Loose what rightfully belongs to me, in Jesus' Name. May every hindrance in the spirit realm be cut down by Your sword of fire Eternal God. I command the promises of God to come forth now. I pray that the gates of heaven will be opened so that the glory of the Lord may be ushered into my spirit. Christ Jesus, connect my heart to Your heart, connect my mind to Your mind, and may my spirit be connected to the core of who You are. Today I submit my will to Your will. In Christ Jesus' Name I pray. Amen.

Day 1: Be Encouraged

You are not just flesh and blood; you also have a spirit. You have power! Like Adam and Eve, we are all born with divine spiritual DNA. It is in the original design of man, so no one is without it. Being made in the image and likeness of God, we don't just physically carry His attributes, but in our spirits we carry a small portion of all of who God is. Humanity spiritually resembles God. Yet do not be confused there is nobody like God and no man is equal to God.

>Genesis 1:26 "Then God said, "Let us make man in our image, in our likeness."

In part, this is the way *The American Heritage Dictionary* defines the following words:

- Likeness: "1. Similarity; resemblance, 2. An imitative appearance, semblance, 3. A copy or picture of something; image.[8]

- Image in noun form as "1. The reproduction of the form of a person or object esp. sculpted likeness. 3. One that closely resembles another.[9]

This is an example. It's like having a two-liter bottle of fruit punch and pouring it from the bottle into a glass.

Now that the fruit punch is in a glass as opposed to the original two-liter bottle it came in, it doesn't change the fact that it is still fruit punch. Even though you can't fit that entire two-liter bottle into that one glass, still a small portion of every ingredient the drink consist of is now in that smaller glass. God has released over 7 billion small portions of Himself, and we are in the earth. That is a lot of power and potential walking around. This reveals just how powerful and not powerless we are as a creation and as individuals. No one exists without a small portion of the essence (attributes) of God within them. The thing is, we need a relationship with the Living God. Knowing the essence of God and having a personal relationship with Him are two different things. The essence of God was given at the beginning, it will never be taken away, relationship with God has always been a choice (free will). Relationship is what makes you a child of God.

Through Christ Jesus' blood, you are spiritual royalty. By the laws set in place by the Almighty God, you have the right to speak and manifest change. Use your authority! Speak into existence whatever you want to see in your future. Don't worry about how things look right now. Throughout this journey, you will learn the value of speaking things that are not as though they already were. That is how God operates. Say what you want, not what you don't want. Even when it seems against all hope, you will train yourself to believe, thereby pleasing God through faith. Don't just have faith that a particular situation will turn around. Rather, have faith in who God is and that His Word is true. **(See. Psalms 33:4)** If He said it, then it will come to pass.

Romans 4:17–18 The God who gives life to the dead and calls those things that are not as though they already were (NIV).

Hebrews 11:6 And without faith it is impossible to please God, because anyone who comes to him must believe that he exists and he rewards those who earnestly seek him (NIV).

Romans 4:18 Against all hope, Abraham believed and so became the father of many nations….(NIV)

Romans 4:20-21 Yet he did not waver through unbelief regarding the promise of God, but was strengthened in his faith and gave glory to God, being fully persuaded that God had power to do what he had promised (NIV).

Whenever we speak, we are coming into agreement with something; we are always creating. What are your words coming into agreement with? Your confession no matter how minor it may seem; gives something open access into your life. What have you given access to enter into your heart, spirit, mind, and future? God's will or something else? What you continuously say, you begin to believe, and what you believe will shape how you live. Prayer is how we communicate with Christ Jesus and the kingdom of heaven. Prayer is something that should be part of our everyday life. Christ Jesus wants us to use our mouth to call forth what He has ordained.

Prayer is something we can do verbally and in the heart. When you go to God in prayer, share whatever is on your heart. God is looking forward to hearing from you and spending time with you. Remember that pursuing God and His promises is a lifetime commitment. Make a decision today to pursue God all the way into eternity. You are never too young to seek God. Today is your day!

Day 1: Today's Goal

Make it a point today to speak only positive things over yourself and others. If you don't desire to see a particular event happen in your future, don't speak it into existence. As you put this into practice, it will become natural.

Day 1: From Your Own Perspective

Which areas of your life do you need to change your confession over?

_____

_____

What can you say today that will manifest a divine change in your life?

_____

_____

Day 1: Daily Journal

DAY 2: The God Encounter

Today's Confession
Read Aloud

I decree and declare that I am attentive and alert to the movements of heaven. I open my soul to the frequencies of the throne room of the Eternal God. I will have a divine encounter with Christ Jesus.

Day 2: Bread for the Soul

Genesis 5:22–24 And after he became the Father of Methuselah, Enoch walked with God 300 years and had other sons and daughters. Altogether, Enoch lived 365 years. Enoch walked with God, and then he was no more, because God took him away (NIV).

Genesis 18:1–3 The Lord appeared to Abraham near the great trees of Mamre while he was sitting at the entrance to his tent in the heat of the day. Abraham looked up and saw three men standing nearby. When he saw them, he hurried from the entrance of his tent to meet them and bowed low to the ground. He said, "If I have found favor in your eyes, my lord, do not pass your servant by (NIV).

Exodus 3:1–6 Now Moses was tending the flock of Jethro his father-in-law, the priest of Midian, and he led the flock to the far side of the desert and came to Horeb, the mountain of God. There the angel of the Lord appeared to him in the flames of fire from within a bush. Moses saw that though the bush was on fire, it did not burn up. So Moses thought, "I will go over and see this strange sight, why the bush does not burn up." When the Lord saw that he had gone over to look, God called to him from within the bush, "Moses! Moses!" And Moses said, "Here I am." "Do not come any closer," God said. "Take off your sandals, for the place where you are standing is holy ground." Then he said, "I am the God of your father, the God of Abraham, the God of Isaac, and the God of Jacob." At this, Moses hid his face, because he was afraid to look at God (NIV).

2 Kings 6:8–17 Now the king of Aram was at war with Israel. After conferring with his officers, he said, "I will set up my camp in such and such a place." The man of God sent word to the king of Israel: "Beware of passing that place because the Arameans are going down there." So the king of Israel checked on the place indicated by the man of God. Time and again, Elisha warned the king so that he was on his guard in such places. This enraged the king of Aram. He summoned his officers and demanded of them, "Will you not tell me which of us is on the side of the king of Israel?" "None of us, my lord the king," said one of his officers, "but Elisha, the prophet who is in Israel, tells the king of Israel the very words you speak in your bedroom." "Go find out where he is," the king ordered, "so I can send men and capture him." The report came back: "He is in Dothan." Then he sent horses and chariots and a strong force there. They went by night and surrounded the city. When the servant of the man of God got up and went out early the next morning, an army with horses and chariots had surrounded the city. "Oh, my lord, what shall we do?" the servant asked. "Don't be afraid," the prophet answered. "Those who are with us are more than those who are with them." And Elisha prayed, "O Lord, open his eyes so he may see." Then the Lord opened the servant's eyes, and he looked and saw the hills full of horses and chariots of fire all around Elisha (NIV).

Day 2: Today's Prayer
Read Aloud

Christ Jesus, I thank You this day and for Your love. God of Israel, I know that even now you are still working and planning on behalf of your children. Christ Jesus, I pray that as I grow in my relationship with You, my soul will draw closer to where You are. Lord, awaken me to the sound of Your voice. Christ Jesus, I pray for visions and dreams from Your right hand. Inform me, Lord of heavens, of Your next move and how I can take part. Lord, let my spirit be sensitive to every shift You make in the spirit realm. Christ Jesus, open my spiritual eyes and allow me to see the presence of Your glory around me. Lord, when You call hearings in Your royal court, let my soul catch but a word from Your lips. Take me higher in You, God. Let me walk with You as Enoch did. Come visit me as You did with Abraham. God, let me have a divine encounter with You as Moses did. Christ Jesus, take me to the secret place with You as You took Peter, James, and John. **(Matthew 17:1-3)** Lord, I am asking You for Your favor. Holy Spirit, prompt me when I need to tune into heaven's dialogue. God speaks to those who are willing to listen. God of

Israel, I'm here. Speak to me. Christ Jesus, I open my soul to You; may I have daily supernatural experiences with Your glory. In Christ Jesus' Name I pray. Amen.

Day 2: Be Encouraged

Christ Jesus is no myth, and the Kingdom of God is not a fairy tale. God is real. There is a greater reality than the one we experience on a daily basis, and that is the spirit realm. Whether good or bad, when events happen on Earth, know that there is a billion times more activity going on at the spiritual level. What you have to decide as an individual is which kingdom in the spirit realm you will serve. We are all connected to something that is beyond what the natural eye can see, and our daily actions decide what we are connected to. Everyone's life, whether they believe in God or not, gives glory to someone or something. That can be good or bad.

This book is about more than just confessions; it will teach you to fight back. As a young person, you may face attacks from the kingdom of darkness. But don't be afraid; through Christ Jesus, your battle is already won. The Word of God is your sword, and it was given to you for reason. In this book, you will see examples of prayer, using the Word of God. The Bible teaches you how to combat the enemy's tricks. Take authority in the spirit realm first, and then watch that same authority manifest in the natural. But to have victory, you must become active and intentional in your prayer life and walk with God. You have a say over your sphere of influence, including the one beyond this world.

God wants to show you something greater than what any fable can ever tell you. Christ Jesus sits at the right hand of God. The realms of God are more real than the air you breathe. Climb higher. To do this, you need to welcome Christ Jesus in and keep walking with Him. The war between good and evil has existed before the ages began. Today, decide which army you fight for. Decide with whom you will take up arms. Make a decision today that you will not quit. Take the oath before Christ Jesus. Tell God, "Even in the face of dire circumstances, God, I will follow You into battle once more." Sometimes all God needs from us is the decision that we are willing believe one more time. Christ Jesus is always before you. You are never alone.

Day 2: Today's Goal

Today cut out 30 minutes of your time and give it to God. If you would normally, watch T.V. or play video games during that time go speak with God. Simply ask, "God what are You doing?" You may be surprised at the answer.

Day 2: From Your Own Perspective

If Christ Jesus were standing right in front you, what would you say?

_____
_____
_____
_____
_____

What aspect of God's kingdom do you want Him to reveal to you?

_____
_____
_____
_____
_____
_____

Day 2: Daily Journal

DAY 3: God's Love

Today's Confession
Read Aloud

I decree and declare that I love Christ Jesus with all my heart, my mind, my strength, and all that I am. I know and accept that Christ Jesus loves me unconditionally and forever.

Day 3: What It Means to Be and What Is

- Heart: 2. The vital center and source of one's being, feelings, emotions.[10]

Love God from the core, from the essence of life within you. Just as the physical heart pumps blood into the rest of the body, loving God from the heart allows Him to release the flow of His Spirit into every area of your life. The body needs the heart to live; the soul needs the Spirit of Christ Jesus to survive.

Day 3: Bread for the Soul

Romans 5:8 But God demonstrates his own love for us in this: While we were still sinners, Christ died for us (NIV).

Romans 8:38–39 For I am convinced that neither death nor life, neither angels nor demons, neither present nor the future, nor any powers, neither height nor depth, nor anything else in all creation, will be able to separate us from the love of God that is in Christ Jesus our Lord (NIV).

1 John 4:9–10 This is how God showed his love among us: He sent his one and only Son into the world that we might live through him. This is love: not that we loved God, but that he loved us and sent his Son as an atoning sacrifice for our sins (NIV).

John 3:16–18 For God so loved the world that he gave his one and only Son, that whoever believes in him shall not perish but have eternal life. For God did not send his Son into the world to condemn the world, but to save the world through him. Whoever believes in him is not condemned, but whoever does not believe stands condemned already because he has not believed in the name of God's one and only Son (NIV).

Day 3: Today's Prayer
Read Aloud

Christ Jesus, I thank You for bringing me into Your presence. I thank You for the unconditional love You have for me. Jesus, I thank You for the cross and for shedding Your blood that I may live. Help me never to doubt Your love for me. Christ Jesus, may Your love rest upon me like heaven's dew. Christ Jesus, in accordance with **Ezekiel 11:19–20**, please give me an undivided heart and put a new spirit within me. Remove from me a heart of stone, and give me a heart of flesh. Then I will follow Your decrees and be careful to keep Your laws. I will be Yours, and You will be my God. Lord, let my confidence in You be fortified by Your blood. Christ Jesus, saturate my inner man with Your healing power. I give You thanks this day for blessing humanity with a greater promise. This was Your perfect will. In Christ Jesus' Name I pray. Amen.

Day 3: Be Encouraged

Jesus Christ came into the world to save each one of us from our sins. When Jesus died on the cross, He had you in mind. Christ Jesus' love for you will never change. There is nothing you can do to step outside of the realms of God's love. God knew all the mistakes that you and I would make in our lifetime, but guess what? He died anyway. You have a heavenly Father who watches over you. Sometimes as humans, no matter how old or young, we question God's love because of the troubles we face. I want you to know that trouble is not the absence of God; rather it is an opportunity to overcome and be victorious through Christ Jesus. Most people have at least one superhero in their life—for example, their mom or dad. Superheroes seem to swoop in and save the day when things are at their worst. Christ Jesus is the best superhero, and He is real. He saved all of us over 2,000 years ago before we came face to face with our troubles. I want you to know that, no matter how bad your situation may be, God is still the ultimate superhero, and He will come for you. Christ Jesus loves us more than our moms, dads, or any other human being ever could. Don't ever give up on Christ Jesus or yourself. You have a heavenly Father who longs to save the day. If you remember nothing else today, know that you are loved.

Day 3: Today's Goal

As you go about your day, meditate on God's love for you. Ask Christ Jesus to wrap His love around your heart and spirit today. Pick out one character trait of God's love, and share that with someone else.

Day 3: From Your Own Perspective

How has Christ Jesus shown His love in your own life?

_____
_____
_____
_____
_____
_____

How will you show your love for God today?

_____
_____
_____
_____

Even when God corrects you, do you understand that He still loves you?

Proverbs 3:11-12 My son, do not despise the Lords discipline and do not resent his rebuke, because the Lord disciplines those he loves, as a father the son he delights in (NIV).

Hebrews 12:5-6 "My son do not make light of the Lords discipline, and do not lose heart when he rebukes you, because the Lord disciplines those he loves.....(NIV)

Also See. **Hebrews 12:4-12**

_____
_____
_____
_____
_____

Day 3: Daily Journal

DAY 4: Better Than Sacrifice

Today's Confession
Read Aloud

I decree and declare I am obedient, cooperative, and respectful.

Day 4: What It Means to Be and What Is

- Obedient: Dutifully complying with the orders or instructions of one in authority.[11]

- Cooperate: To work together for a common end.[12]

- Cooperative: Willing to cooperate.[13]

- Respect: To have regard for; esteem.[14]

Day 4: Bread for the Soul

Galatians 5:22-23 But the fruit of the Spirit is love, joy, peace, patience, kindness, goodness, faithfulness, gentleness, and self-control (NIV).

1 Samuel 15:22 But Samuel replied: Does the Lord delight in burnt offerings and sacrifices as much as in obeying the voice of the Lord? To obey is better than sacrifice and to heed is better than the fat of rams (NIV).

1 Samuel 15:23 "For rebellion is as the sin of witchcraft, and stubbornness is as iniquity and idolatry (KJV)."

Ephesians 6:1–3 Children, obey your parents in the Lord, for this is right. "Honor your father and mother"—which is the first commandment with a promise—"that it may go well with you and that you may enjoy long life on earth" (NIV).

John 14:15–17 If you love me, you will obey what I command. And I will ask the Father, and He will give you another Counselor to be with you forever—the Spirit of truth (NIV).

Day 4: Today's Prayer
Read Aloud

Lord, I thank You for this day and for all of Your blessings. Christ Jesus, I thank You for the grace to walk in obedience to those in authority over me. Whether I am at school or at home, Lord, quicken my spirit to walk uprightly before You in my actions. Lord, let me be a joy and a light to those You have put over me. Please grant me a humble spirit. Jesus Christ I decree and declare that I will walk in obedience to Your precepts and commands all the days of my life. God of Israel, help me to practice self-control. Lord, I know that, as it says in **2 Peter 1:3**, Your divine power has given me everything I need for life and godliness through my knowledge of You, who called me by Your own glory and goodness (NIV). Jesus, let the grace You have granted Your people to make divine beneficial decisions be manifested in me this day. I will obey You Lord. In Christ Jesus' Name I pray. Amen.

Day 4: Be Encouraged

God requires something of all human beings, regardless of their age, and that is obedience. As you grow in the Lord, you will learn that the best way to live your life is being in right standing with God. Whatever you do, do it unto God. Sometimes life presents temptations or routes other than what God has ordained for us. That's when the power of free will comes into play. In the moments when you are faced with a decision, you have the power to make a divine one. Good decisions manifest supernatural benefits, even if we don't see those benefits right away.

Being obedient to your parents or to those in authority over you is something you do, not only because a person wants you to but also because that's what God requires of you. Live your life beyond the expectations of people, and strive every day to meet the expectations of God. In **1 Samuel 15:22–23**, Samuel told Saul that it was better to do what God asked the first time, or to do right in the first place, than to compensate for disobedience. We no longer sacrifice animals to atone for our sins; Jesus paid the price once and for all by shedding His blood on Calvary. There is a lesson we can take from what Samuel said: "To obey is better than sacrifice." (**1 Samuel 15:23**) Whenever any of us goes against what God requires, we risk sacrificing the benefits of obedience. Let's say, for example, that Mom says to come straight home from school instead of hanging out with friends. Let's say you decide to do as your mom asked, and when you get home, to your surprise, your mom takes you to get that new video game or a new pair of sneakers. Through that one act of obedience, you gained a benefit. Not only did you receive a blessing that day, but your mom can trust you to do what she asks of you the first time. In the future, she may not mind if you hang out an extra ten minutes after school. However, if you had decided to hang out with friends instead of coming straight home, you would have sacrificed the benefits of obedience.

It is the same thing with God. God doesn't like to see His children be delayed blessings or go through unnecessary trouble because of disobedience. Make a decision to walk in obedience not just for materialistic things but for the spiritual blessings and promises that

God has attached to actions and to a lifestyle of obedience. Obedience is something we all work at every single day. When those big and small decisions are in front of you, know that you have the power inside you to make the right choice. Listen to that little voice inside that says, "Walk in the way of the Lord" or "Do what's right."

If you need help, just ask. It's as simple as saying, "Holy Spirit, I need You." As you practice obedience, it becomes a habit, and habits become a lifestyle. One day, you will look up and realize that obedience comes to you just as easily as the air you breathe. Obedience is a way of showing your love for God. Today is a new day; begin again. Tell God, "Regardless of what I want to do, Lord, I love You more than my desire."

Day 4: Today's Goal

For every hour you are awake today, complete three obedient acts. Those acts can manifest in many different ways. For example being quiet in class when asked to or unloading the dishwasher. No act of obedience is small, God takes note of it all. Go out of your way today to find opportunities to be obedient.

Day 4: From Your Own Perspective

What can you do to be obedient to a parent or guardian today?

_____
_____
_____
_____
_____

How can you show cooperation in the classroom?

_____
_____
_____
_____

What does respect mean, and how will you show it today?

_____
_____
_____
_____

Day 4: Daily Journal

DAY 5: Leadership

Today's Confession
Read Aloud

I decree and declare that I am a powerful and effective leader. My leadership skills will open divine doors for me.

Day 5: What It Means to Be and What Is

- Lead: 1. To guide, conduct, escort, or direct. 3. To be ahead or be at the head of.[15]

- Effect: 1. Something brought about by a cause or agent; result. 2. The power to achieve a result; influence.[16]

Day 5: Bread for the Soul

Psalm 25:5 Guide me in your truth and teach me, for you are God my Savior, and my hope is in you all day long (NIV).

Psalm 31:3–5 Since you are my rock and my fortress, for the sake of your name, lead me and guide me. Free me from the trap that is set for me, for you are my refuge. Into your hands I commit my spirit; redeem me, O Lord, the God of truth (NIV).

Psalm 43:3 Send forth your light and your truth, let them guide me; let them bring me to your holy mountain, to the place where you dwell (NIV).

John 16:13 But when he, the Spirit of truth comes, he will guide you into all truth (NIV).

Day 5: Today's Prayer
Read Aloud

Christ Jesus, I thank You for Your blessings this day. Lord, just as You anointed Moses and David, anoint me to be a leader in Your Kingdom. I pray that I will lead others in positive ways by the life that I live. I decree and declare that my life is a testimony of God's Kingdom. Lord, I come against negative influences, right now in Jesus' Name, I tear down every stronghold of peer pressure through the blood of the Lamb. Lord, I understand that my lifestyle is my ministry. As people watch me, Lord, may You be pleased as I exude righteousness. You have commanded me in **1 Peter 1:16** to be holy because You are holy (NIV). So I decree and declare that I will take a stand for the Name of Jesus. I pray that the Holy Spirit will guide me so that I know when to say yes and when to say no. When trouble seen and unseen is ahead, Lord Jesus, may Your grace turn me in the opposite direction. Jesus Christ, manifest the characteristics of a great leader inside of me; so I may meet Your standards and not the standards of this world. I know the greatest leaders are those who submit to Your will. In Christ Jesus' Name I pray. Amen.

Day 5: Be Encouraged

There are great leaders in the bible, including David, Joseph, Esther, Moses, Abraham, and so many more. The greatest leader of all was Jesus Christ. These leaders all had one thing in common: they cared more about God being pleased with them, than people's opinion. Jesus cared more about God being pleased with Him than about being accepted by the "in" crowd. Today, peer pressure is all around us—in school, in the media, and sometimes just walking on the street. Becoming a leader in the kingdom of God is making the choice to take a stand. That stand sometimes occurs through what we say, but the greatest stand we can take comes through how we live.

Moses took a stand when God sent Him to lead the Israelites out of Egypt. Moses had to stand through adversity, but He didn't give up. Moses faced adversity not only from the Egyptians but from the very people God sent him to help **(See. Exodus chapters 3–14)**. Esther took a stand when the Jews were about to be harmed **(See. Esther chapters 3–8)**. David took one of the greatest stands any human being could take by walking in love toward Saul, who tried more than once to take David's life. (See. **1 Samuel chapters 24 and 26**).

All of these people took a stand through the Spirit of God and according to His will. Today, God is looking for individuals who don't mind being different. God is looking for people who will take this walk with Him to the next level. Christ Jesus is looking for people who will pursue in Him and boldly say, "No", when the in crowd says, "Yes" to what is against the will of God. You are a leader. Allow God to shape and mold you into what He says a leader should be. In your friendships and everyday social interactions, influence people in the right way. Don't be swayed by people's reactions. Whether it's a friend or a relative, someone is always watching you. Let your life be a testimony to the work that God is doing in you. God didn't create followers; you were born to lead. Humanity was given the power to rule. Rise and take your rightful place in the earth and in the Kingdom of God. Lead!

Day 5: Today's Goal

At some point today, take a stand. If you see friends doing something wrong, walk away. If you see someone being picked on or sitting alone, go and keep them company. Take the lead today!

Day 5: From Your Own Perspective

What does being a great leader mean to you?

_____
_____
_____
_____
_____
_____

How do you think Christ Jesus wants you to exercise your leadership? In what areas can you do so?

_____
_____
_____
_____

Who do you consider a positive leader in your life, and why?

_____
_____
_____
_____
_____
_____

Day 5: Daily Journal

DAY 6: Understanding

Today's Confession
Read Aloud

I decree and declare that I am smart, spiritually intelligent, and an academic genius. I excel in all my studies. I carry wisdom of the Kingdom of God inside me.

Day 6: What It Means to Be and What Is

- Smart: Intelligent; bright.[17]

- Intelligent: 1a. The capacity to acquire and apply knowledge. 1c. Superior power of mind.[18]

- Genius: 1a. Extraordinary intellectual and creative power. 3. The distinctive character of a place, person, or era.[19]

Day 6: Bread for the Soul

Proverbs 9:10 The fear of the Lord is the beginning of wisdom, and knowledge of the Holy One is understanding (NIV).

Proverbs 4:5–9 Get wisdom, get understanding; do not forget my words or swerve from them. Do not forsake wisdom, and she will protect you; love her, and she will watch over you. Wisdom is supreme; therefore get wisdom. Though it cost all you have, get understanding. Esteem her, and she will exalt you; embrace her, and she will honor you. She will set a garland of grace on your head and present you with a crown of splendor (NIV).

Proverbs 24:3–4 By wisdom a house is built, and through understanding it is established; through knowledge its rooms are filled with rare and beautiful treasures (NIV).

Psalm 111:10 The fear of the Lord is the beginning of wisdom; all who follow his precepts have good understanding. To him belongs eternal praise (NIV).

Daniel 1:17 To these four young men God gave knowledge and understanding of all kinds of literature and learning. And Daniel could understand visions and dreams of all kinds (NIV).

1 Kings 3:11 and 12 So God said to him….. "I will give you a wise and discerning heart, so that there will never have been anyone like you, nor will there ever be (NIV).

1 Kings 4:29-30, 32-34 God gave Solomon wisdom and very great insight, and a breadth of understanding as measureless as the sand on the seashore. Solomon's wisdom was greater than the wisdom of all the men of the East, and greater than all the wisdom of Egypt. He spoke three thousand proverbs and his songs numbered a thousand and five. He described plant life, from the cedar of Lebanon to the hyssop that grows out of the walls. He also taught about animals and birds, reptiles and fish. Men of all nations came to listen to Solomon's wisdom, sent by all the kings of the world, who had heard of his wisdom (NIV).

Day 6: Today's Prayer
Read Aloud

Christ Jesus, God of all things, I come to You thanking You for Your love. Lord, I praise You forever because You are God. Christ Jesus, I pray that You will reveal the secrets of Your Kingdom to me. Lord, I pray that knowledge will come not only through what I see or hear but also in the personal experience of Your majesty. Jesus, Your word says in **James 1:5** "If any of you lacks wisdom, he should ask God, who gives generously to all without finding fault, and it will be given to him (NIV)." God, please reveal to me the secrets of Your love and things that have not yet been made known to man. Lord, bless me with ideas and inventions that will not only cause me to excel but also bring glory to Your Name. Christ Jesus, I decree and declare that the knowledge You have given me shall forever remain pure through Your blood and be used only for good. Jesus Christ, help me in my studies to grasp information quickly and with complete understanding. Lord, as I sit in my classroom, please help my mind to digest the information presented to me. Lord, unlock the gift of comprehension in me. I pray for great success in my studies. I pray for good grades on my report cards and for the diligence to see it come to pass. I decree and declare I have a bright academic future. Lord give me favor with my instructors. Jesus, give me understanding of science, nature, math, history, grammar and the realms of the

Living God. Teach me, Lord, how to speak the language of God. May I uplift others with the wisdom I acquire. Give me opportunities to share the knowledge of Your Kingdom with the world. Let everyone who hears me speak come to repentance through Your salvation, Christ Jesus. In Jesus' Name I pray. Amen.

Day 6: Be Encouraged

People express their intelligence in so many different ways. The type of intelligence one person has another may not have, and vice versa. For example, a painter expresses intelligence in portraying with a paintbrush what he sees. A dancer expresses intelligence through movement. A singer expresses intelligence through the sound of his/her voice. A musician expresses intelligence by playing an instrument. A scientist expresses intelligence through invention and experiments. We are all intelligent.

God wants you to know that He has hidden amazing things in you that will be revealed. We talked earlier about divine spiritual DNA. You have not only a physical mind but also a spiritual place inside where information is obtained. You have spiritual genetic information (DNA) as well as physical DNA. DNA is where information is stored.

- DNA: A nucleic acid that carries the genetic information[20]

There is eternal wisdom stored in you, and the Holy Spirit wants you to know that there is no issue He can't help you with. The Holy Spirit can help your understanding to go deeper in any school subject. The next time you have trouble, ask God to help your physical mind to understand, but also ask Him to help Your spirit to understand. When God gave Solomon wisdom, He imparted it not just in his mind but in his spirit. God gave insight to Solomon in ways that no other human on earth experienced. When the bible says that Solomon had understanding of nature, that knowledge didn't come from a book; it was downloaded directly by the hand of God. **(See 1 Kings 4:29–34.)**

The next scriptures speak of who Christ Jesus is. The Bible says in **Colossians 1:15–17**, "He is the image of the invisible God, the firstborn over all creation. For by him all things were created: things in heaven and on earth, visible and invisible, whether thrones or powers or rulers or authorities; all things were created by him and for him. He is before all things, and in him all things hold together" (NIV). God always has something more, so open your spirit to listen. Do not simply imagine that you will be someone when you grow up; you are someone right now. Your worth goes beyond what this world could ever measure. God wants you to apply your best effort to your studies. God is not searching for perfection; He is looking for consistency and your very best. That applies to every area of your life, not just school. The knowledge and gifts that Christ Jesus has extended to you sets you apart. You are unique. You are great and have a profound mind.

Day 6: Today's Goal

Pick your favorite subject in school. When you go home today, ask God to reveal something new about it to you. In addition, seek God's purpose for the existence of that particular subject. Remember, God always has a plan for everything He creates and reveals.

Day 6: From Your Own Perspective

What subject in school do you need God's help in? Have you informed God of the areas where you need assistance? God uses the natural things to help up along. So don't be afraid to utilize the tools He has put in front of you for example, tutoring.

_____
_____
_____
_____
_____

What things in God's creation capture your interest?

_____
_____
_____
_____
_____
_____

What will you do today to learn more about God?

_____
_____
_____
_____
_____
_____

Day 6: Daily Journal

DAY 7: Potential

Today's Confession
Read Aloud

I decree and declare that through the blood and salvation of Christ Jesus, I am powerful beyond the measure of the sands on the seashore. I will exercise that power within the will of Christ Jesus. I am armed and ready for battle through the Spirit of the Living God.

Day 7: What It Means To Be and What Is

- Power: 1. The ability or capacity to perform or act effectively. 3. Strength or force exerted or capable of being exerted; might.[21]

- Measure: 1. Dimensions, quantities, or capacity ascertained by a standard. 2. A reference used for the quantitative comparison of properties.[22]

Day 7: Bread for the Soul

1 John 4:4 Ye are of God, little children, and have overcome them: because greater is he that is in you, than he that is in the world (KJV).

Ephesians 6:10–18 Finally, be strong in the Lord and in his mighty power. Put on the whole armor of God so that you can take your stand against the devil's schemes. For our struggle is not against flesh and blood but against the rulers, against the authorities, against the powers of this dark world, and against the spiritual forces of evil in the heavenly realms. Therefore, put on the full armor of God so that when the day of evil comes, you will be able to stand your ground, and after you have done everything, to stand. Stand firm then, with the belt of truth buckled around your waist, with the breastplate of righteousness in place, and with your feet fitted with the readiness that comes from the gospel of peace. In addition to all this, take up the shield of faith, with which you can extinguish all the flaming arrows of the evil one. Take the helmet of salvation and the sword of the Spirit, which is the Word of God. And pray in the Spirit on all occasions with all kinds of prayers and requests. With this in mind, be alert and always keep on praying for all the saints (NIV).

Luke 10:19 I have given you authority to trample on snakes and scorpions and to overcome all the power of the enemy; nothing will harm you (NIV).

Romans 8:11 But if the Spirit of Him that raised up Jesus from the dead dwell in you, he that raised up Christ from the dead shall also quicken your mortal bodies by His Spirit that dwelleth in you (KJV).

Day 7: Today's Prayer
Read Aloud

Christ Jesus, I thank You for Your prayers that You have offered up for me. I praise You because You are God. I thank You, Lord, that I am created in Your image and likeness. God, You created me to rule. I refute the words "I can't" through the blood of Jesus. I know that I can do all things through Christ who strengthens me **(Philippians 4:13)**. Lord, I turn the power in me over to Your will. Lord, I command my spirit to align itself with You. I speak to every dormant area of my life that You have ordained to live, commanding them to become alive. Just as Ezekiel did in the valley, I prophesy to the dry bones in my life and command them to hear the Word that God has spoken over my life **(Ezekiel 37:4)**. Remembering **Ezekiel 37:9**, right now I speak into the atmosphere; I welcome the four winds of heaven to breathe life into the slain areas of my heart and life that God has ordained to live. God, breathe life into my destiny, into my purpose. I command the gifts that God has placed inside of me to come to life in Jesus' Name. Jesus, kindle a fire in me that cannot be quenched. I speak to the territories God has given me in the spirit realm. I call on the fire of the living God to sweep through my land and purify the atmosphere. Christ Jesus, I pray that Your hand will reach into the soil of my spirit and my mind, uprooting every evil seed. I disrupt the plans of the enemy though the blood of Jesus Christ. I call forth the holy angels to do warfare on my behalf. I decree and declare that the power God has given me to reach new heights and levels in Him is being unleashed. I am no longer a product of this world; I am made new. Through the blood of Jesus, I command the kingdom of darkness to drop everything that belongs to me. I decree and declare that God's wind of judgment is blowing into the enemy's camp at this very moment in Jesus' Name. I send forth a divine spiritual tornado directed by the finger of Yahweh to destroy the barracks that the adversary has tried to set up in my life. Lord, as You did in **Exodus 10:19**, please send a very strong west wind and drive every locust in my life into the sea; let it never resurface again. You have given me authority, God, and I exercise it through Your Word this day. Today I am victorious. In Christ Jesus' Name I pray. Amen.

Day 7: Be Encouraged

Power can be either divine or diabolical. Divine power operates within the realms of God's will. Diabolical power is used outside of God's will and is called witchcraft or manipulation. All of us have God-given power within us, and we decide to whom or what we will submit our power. Whatever you submit your power to has power over you.

You have the power to create, build, inspire, and so much more. You have the power to do spiritual warfare in your prayer closet every single day. God has given you power over the kingdom of darkness and its tricks. That's a battle Jesus Christ won long ago. Walk in it!

One of our most powerful tools is free will. Free will is the choice to do right or wrong. When power and free will meet, we decide at that moment whether that power is divine or diabolical. With every decision you make, you are exercising power. It's not possible for any human being to exercise the full potential of the power inside them outside of Christ Jesus. No matter what something looks like on the outside, all things are incomplete and obsolete outside of the will of the Christ Jesus. The power in you cannot be measured or fathomed by humanity because it is from God. Never let anyone tell you what you are *not* capable of. You can do *anything*. What is in you is immeasurable.

Day 7: Today's Goal

Identify moments of power in your own life today. As you go throughout the day, identify choices and opt to make divine decisions. Make a conscious choice to use that power to the glory of Christ Jesus.

Day 7: From Your Own Perspective

In what areas of your life do you want to exercise divine power through Christ Jesus?

_____
_____
_____
_____
_____
_____

What are you going to do to take back power in certain areas you feel you may have lost?

_____
_____
_____
_____
_____

Day 7: Daily Journal

Day 8: My Identity

Today's sections are broken down into two parts. There is a section for young gentlemen and another section for young ladies.

DAY 8: God's Prince

Today's Confession
(For Young Gentlemen) *Read Aloud*

I decree and declare that I am handsome, chivalrous, a mighty man of valor, chaste, noble, a warrior before the Lord, and a prince in the Kingdom of the Living God.

Day 8: What It Means to Be and What Is

- Handsome: Pleasing and dignified in form or appearance.[23]

- Chivalry: Qualities such as bravery, honor, and gallantry toward women.[24]

- Mighty: 1. Having great power. 2. Imposing or awesome.[25]

- Valor: Courage and boldness, as in battle or bravery.[26]

- Chaste: Morally pure; modest.[27]

- Nobility: A class of persons distinguished by high birth or rank.[28]

- Noble: Having or showing high moral character.[29]

- Warrior: One engaged or experienced in battle.[30]

- Prince: 1. A boy or a man in a royal family. 3. An outstanding man in a group or class.[31]

Day 8: Bread for the Soul

1 Peter 2:9 But you are a chosen people, a royal priesthood, a holy nation, a people belonging to God, that you may declare the praises of him who called you out of darkness into his wonderful light (NIV).

Judges 6:12 And the angel of the Lord appeared unto him and said unto him, The Lord is with thee, thou mighty man of valour (KJV).

Jeremiah 20:11 But the Lord is with me like a mighty warrior... (NIV).

Psalm 139:14–16 I praise you because I am fearfully and wonderfully made; your works are wonderful, I know that full well. My frame was not hidden from you when I was made in the secret place. When I was woven together in the depths of the earth, your eyes saw my unformed body. All the days ordained for me were written in your book before one of them came to be (NIV).

Day 8: Today's Prayer
Read Aloud

Christ Jesus, I thank You for who I am. I give You glory, Lord, for creating me. Lord, as a male, I accept the mandate to be the head. Jesus, I pray that You will teach me to be a mighty warrior before You, tearing down the kingdom of darkness through prayer and supplication. I know, Father, that we fight not with the weapons of this world but through God we are pulling down strongholds (**2 Corinthians** 10:4). Christ Jesus, mold me into what You hold a true man to be. Lord, I just ask heaven to grant me divine masculinity through the Holy Spirit. Christ Jesus, as a prince in Your Kingdom, I will walk uprightly before You. Lord, let my spirit carry the aroma of divine royalty and of Your heart. Dip my spirit in the oils of the kingdom of heaven. God, You are King of kings and Lord of lords. Lord, may I ever pursue You. Jesus, help me to be one who is truly after God's own heart. Help me to always respect myself and others. I will walk in purity before You, Christ Jesus. I pray that You will delight in my worship. As a son, may I always abide in a special place in Your heart. Thank You, Lord, for sharing Your inheritance with me. In Jesus' Name I pray. Amen.

Day 8: Be Encouraged

There are many mighty men in the kingdom of God. Physical height, strength, and even appearance are not what make a man mighty; rather the aroma of his heart determines that. Christ Jesus wants you to know that you are what He is looking for. In the Bible, many men fought wars and battles. God is looking for men today who will be on the frontlines in the spiritual realm, men who will stand for righteousness and for what pleases God. God is looking for men who will promote His original purpose and design for males. You have a heavenly Father, His Name is Jesus and He loves you. As you go throughout this life, allow Christ Jesus to give you discernment. It is a great honor to be a prince in the kingdom of God. As a prince, you are directly connected to God and able to call Him Father, Friend, and King. Real men serve Christ Jesus. Be brave and courageous. Remember, it's what's on the inside that makes you mighty before the Lord. It's your identity in Christ Jesus that makes you a man.

Day 8: Today's Goal

Make an effort today to conduct yourself as royalty by walking in the character of Christ Jesus. Be kind to those around you, and open your heart so the love of God can shine through. Let the grace of God on your life be a royal banner that marks you as a representative of the kingdom of heaven here on earth. Look yourself in the mirror today and say, "I am a mighty man of God." Then look inside your heart and identify three things you love about yourself.

Day 8: From Your Own Perspective

What does it mean to be royalty?

_____
_____
_____
_____

What specific character traits do you want Jesus to produce in you?

_____
_____
_____
_____

Day 8: Daily Journal

DAY 8: God's Princess

Today's Confession
(For Young Ladies) *Read Aloud*

I decree and declare that I am absolutely gorgeous and beautiful inside and out. I am clothed in strength and dignity. I am virtuous. I decree and declare that I am elegant, noble, worth far more than rubies, a treasure, a young lady who fears the Lord, and a princess in the Kingdom of the Living God.

Day 8: What It Means to Be and What Is

- Gorgeous: Dazzling beauty or magnificent.[32]

- Beauty: 1. A quality that pleases or delights the senses or mind. 3. An outstanding example.[33]

- Virtue: Moral excellence and righteousness; goodness. 2. Chastity in a woman.[34]

- Elegance: Refinement and grace in movement, appearance, or manners.[35]

- Nobility: A class of persons distinguished by high birth or rank.[36]

- Noble: Having or showing high moral character.[37]

- Treasure: One considered precious or valuable.[38]

- Princess: A female member of a royal family.[39]

Day 8: Bread for the Soul

Psalm 139:14–16 I praise you because I am fearfully and wonderfully made; your works are wonderful, I know that full well. My frame was not hidden from you when I was made in the secret place. When I was woven together in the depths of the earth, your eyes saw my unformed body. All the days ordained for me were written in your book before one of them came to be (NIV).

Psalm 149:4 For the Lord taketh pleasure in his people: he will beautify the meek with Salvation (KJV).

1 Peter 2:9 But you are a chosen people, a royal priesthood, a holy nation, a people belonging to God, that you may declare the praises of him who called you out of darkness into his wonderful light (NIV).

Proverbs 31:25-26 She is clothed in strength and dignity; she can laugh at the days to come. She speaks with wisdom, and faithful instruction is on her tongue (NIV).

Proverbs 31:30 Charm is deceptive and beauty is fleeting; but a woman who fears the Lord is to be praised (NIV).

Proverbs 24:3-4 By wisdom a house is built, and through understanding it is established; through knowledge its rooms are filled with rare and beautiful treasures (NIV).

Also see. **Proverbs 31:10**

Day 8: Today's Prayer
Read Aloud

Christ Jesus, God of all things, I thank You for Your goodness. I thank You, Lord, for raising up women to be ambassadors in Your Kingdom and preach the gospel of Jesus Christ. Lord, I pray that You will beautify my spirit and heart. I thank You, Christ Jesus, for granting me an attitude and spirit of meekness. Lord, I just ask heaven to grant me divine femininity through the Holy Spirit. Christ Jesus, bring forth in me the characteristics described in Proverbs 31. As a princess in Your kingdom, Lord, I will walk uprightly before You. Christ Jesus, let my spirit carry the aroma of divine royalty and the fragrance of Your heart. Dip my spirit in the oils of the kingdom of heaven. Lord build me through Your wisdom and establish me with understanding of Your will. Through the knowledge of You Christ Jesus; I pray that you will fill my soul with rare and beautiful treasures. God, You are King of kings and Lord of lords. May I ever pursue You. Jesus, help me to be one who is truly after God's own heart. I will be a woman who fears the Lord all the days of my life. Lord, help me to accept my value and grasp the truth that I am a treasure. Lord, help me to always respect myself and others. I will walk in purity before You, Christ Jesus. Lord, I pray that You will delight in my worship. As a daughter, I pray to always rest in a special place in Your heart. Thank You, Lord, for sharing Your inheritance with me. In Christ Jesus' Name I pray. Amen.

Day 8: Be Encouraged

Women are special in God's eyes. You are absolutely gorgeous in the eyes of God. You have a heavenly Father, His Name is Jesus and He loves you. As a young lady, sometimes we are into fashion. We want to have that certain piece of jewelry or clothing to appear a particular way on the outside. Jesus wants you to have the most important accessory of all—an inner beauty that makes you look like Him. Beauty in the kingdom of God is defined beyond what meets the eye. God created beauty. God defined beauty before humanity ever came into existence. As a young lady, accept spiritual beauty from the hands of Christ Jesus. Pursue the likeness of a woman and spirit of femininity from the hands of God. Women are preachers, evangelists, prophets, and so many other things in the kingdom of God. You can become whatever you want to become in this life. Christ Jesus has a great call on your life, and He wants you to know that you are His. You are a treasure in the hands of God.

Day 8: Today's Goal

Make an effort today to conduct yourself as royalty by walking in the character of Christ Jesus. Be kind to those around you, and open your heart so the love of God can shine through. Let the grace of God on your life be a royal banner that marks you as a representative of the kingdom of heaven here on earth. Look yourself in the mirror today and say, "I am absolutely gorgeous and so beautiful." Then look inside your heart and identify three things you love about yourself. Ask the Holy Spirit to reveal to you what true beauty is. As you grow in the Lord, ask Him to make room in your heart so that He can radiate divine, spiritual beauty through you. Beauty from God's hand outshines what humans define as beauty any day.

Day 8: From Your Own Perspective

What does it mean to be royalty?

_____
_____
_____
_____

What does beauty mean to you?

_____
_____
_____
_____
_____

Day 8: Daily Journal

DAY 9: God I Agree

Today's Confession
Read Aloud

I decree and declare that I love and accept myself. I accept who Christ Jesus says I am. From this day forward, I will see myself only as God sees me. I am a holy nation, the head and not the tail, a friend of God, I am the lender and not the borrower.

Day 9: Bread for the Soul

Jeremiah 29:11–14 For I know the plans I have for you, declares the Lord, plans to prosper you and not to harm you, plans to give you a hope and a future. Then you will call upon me and come and pray to me, and I will listen to you. You will seek me and find me when you seek me with all your heart. I will be found by you, declares the Lord (NIV).

Deuteronomy 28:12-14 The Lord will open the heavens, the storehouse of his bounty, to send rain on your land in season and to bless all the work of your hands. You will lend to many nations but will borrow from none. The Lord will make you the head, not the tail. If you pay attention to the commands of the Lord your God that I give you this day and carefully follow them, you will always be at the top and never the bottom. Do not turn aside from any of the commands I give you today, to the right or to the left, following other gods and serving them (NIV).

Psalms 138:8 The Lord will perfect that which concerneth me: thy mercy, O lord, endureth forever: forsake not the works of thine own hands (KJV).

Day 9: Today's Prayer
Read Aloud

Christ Jesus, thank You for Your love and peace. Lord, I thank You that the thoughts You have toward me are thoughts of good. You have chosen me before the foundations of the world, before time existed. Christ Jesus, help me to be confident and to see myself through Your eyes. I bind the spirit of low self-esteem right now in Jesus' Name. It is uprooted in my life and I am free. Lord I thank you that I have very high self-esteem that is established and confirmed in You. Christ Jesus, show me what it means to be Your friend. May You call me a friend as God called Abraham His friend. Let Your Spirit lead me to the place where I do not seek You only for what I can gain; but rather be genuinely interested in the affairs of the heart of the Eternal God. Lord, I understand that my challenges do not mean You are absent. Rather, they are portals of grace to experience more of Your glory. Lord, reveal to me a glimpse of the blueprint that heaven has for my life; put me on the right path to make it to the finish line. Lord, help me to be my very best. In due season, I decree and declare that the greatness You have put in me shall spring forth. I shall become who heaven has ordained me to be. I am a child of the Most High God. In Christ Jesus' Name I pray. Amen.

Day 9: Be Encouraged

As you grow up, many different ideas will be presented to you about who you are and who you are supposed to be. At some point, every human being wants to know why he or she is here on the earth. If anyone ever presents a message to you that goes against what God says about you, reject it. Christ wants you to know that all of who you are and will ever be is in Him. God knows everything about you—even the number of hairs on your head **(Luke 12:7, Matthew 10:30)**. You as the creation can go to the Creator God and ask who you are. The Word of God speaks about who we are to God and how God sees us. *Never* let anyone tell you that you are less than God says you are because that is false. God accepts you, and He wants you to know that you are always welcome in His Kingdom—always.

Sometimes as humans think that having a person reject us means God rejected us, but that's not true at all. While Jesus was on earth, many people rejected Him and did not believe in the message of the kingdom of Heaven. The fact that people rejected Jesus Christ definitely did not mean God rejected Him. God sent Jesus into the world to die for our sins. Sometimes when God sends you to certain places, people may not receive you. But God has not left you, and His purpose for your life will not change. If you have doubt in your own mind about who God says you are, bind those negative thoughts in Jesus' Name. Gain a new perspective when you look in the mirror today. Believe...

Day 9: Today's Goal

Identify one area you believe the Lord will use you in, whether its dance, writing, sports, medicine, cooking, or something else. For the next three days, ask God to reveal to you the direction in which He wants you to walk. Ministry goes beyond church walls. God uses people in all types of fields to bring glory to His Name—in business, arts, culinary arenas, and so on. As you seek God, always put more trust in Him than in the gift itself. So if you are a singer, put more faith in God than in having a good voice. If you are a painter, put more trust in the canvas of God's plan for you than in any portrait you may create. Make Christ Jesus, not an ability, the source of your identity and confidence. As you submit yourself to God, God perfects your gifts and callings.

Day 9: From Your Own Perspective

Who do you want to become in God?

_____
_____
_____
_____
_____

Do you see yourself as God sees you?

_____
_____
_____
_____
_____

How will you give your gifts and talents back to God?

_____
_____
_____
_____
_____

Is there a particular area of self-esteem in which you need Christ Jesus' help? If you tell Him, He is listening.

_____
_____
_____
_____
_____

Day 9: Daily Journal

DAY 10: Favor

Today's Confession
Read Aloud

I decree and declare that the favor of God rests upon my life. I am loved and celebrated by all who come in contact with me.

Day 10: What It Means to Be and What Is

- Favor: 1. A gracious, friendly, or obliging act that is freely granted. 2a. Friendly regard; approval or support.[40]

Day 10: Bread for the Soul

Psalm 5:12 For surely, O Lord, you will bless the righteous; you surround them with favor as a shield (NIV).

Psalm 30:4–5 Sing to the Lord, you saints of his; praise his holy name. For his anger lasts only a moment, but his favor lasts a lifetime; weeping may endure for a night, but rejoicing comes in the morning (NIV).

Proverbs 3:1–4 My son, do not forget my teaching, but keep my commands in your heart, for they will prolong your life many years and bring you prosperity. Let love and faithfulness never leave you; bind them around your neck and write them on the tablet of your heart. Then you will win favor and a good name in the sight of God and man (NIV).

Luke 2:14 Glory to God in the highest, and on earth peace to men on whom his favor rests (NIV).

Day 10: Today's Prayer
Read Aloud

God of Israel, You are greater than any being can fathom. Your Name is to be praised from everlasting to everlasting. Better is one day in Your courts than a thousand elsewhere **(Psalm 40:10).** Lord, You are my comforter and shield; please bestow upon me favor and honor **(Psalm 84:11)**. Christ Jesus, I pray that You will ever intercede for me before the Father and that my spirit may dwell in the worship halls of heaven. Lord, allow me to bow at Your feet and worship You for who You are. Lord, Your favor is priceless and dwells with the righteous. Your favor goes beyond what I can obtain in this life; it is an eternal serum that consumes the soul. Lord, remember me. Show me how to live a life that heaven cannot forget. Christ, You are the Son of the Living God. Let Your favor be with me wherever I go, Lord. In Jesus' Name. Amen.

Day 10: Be Encouraged

God's favor is more precious than life itself. Christ Jesus is King, and resting in the favor of God is an awesome existence. God's favor rests upon humanity. There are so many ways God's favor comes about. Sometimes favor is the very thing we take for granted every single day. It's important to always be thankful for God grace. All of God's grace is magnificent and precious. One way to obtain more favor is to learn of God. As you learn of God, you can begin to walk in His precepts. Obedience opens doors to great favor from God. Favor grants you access to things that not everyone has, so as you live for God, always know you are under the shadow of His grace.

Day 10: Today's Goal

Favor from God goes deep into a person's relationship with Him. Your best friend can probably walk in your room and use anything he or she wants. Your best friend is likely always around. Make time to be around God, to hang out with God. All that He has is yours; take hold of it.

Day 10: From Your Own Perspective

How has God's favor rested upon your life?

_____
_____
_____
_____
_____

How do you want God's favor to rest upon your family or friends?

_____
_____
_____
_____
_____

Day 10: Daily Journal

DAY 11: Stand

Today's Confession
Read Aloud

I decree and declare that I am lionhearted and as innocent as a dove.

Day 11: What It Means to Be and What Is

- Lionhearted: Extraordinarily courageous.[41]

- Innocent: Uncorrupted by evil, malice, or wrongdoing.[42]

Day 11: Bread for the Soul

2 Timothy 1:7 For God hath not given us the spirit of fear; but of power, and of love, and of a sound mind (KJV).

Joshua 1:9 Have I not commanded you? Be strong and courageous. Do not be terrified; do not be discouraged, for the Lord your God will be with you wherever you go (NIV).

Psalm 27:13–14 I am still confident of this: I will see the goodness of the Lord in the land of the living. Wait for the Lord; be strong and take heart and wait for the Lord (NIV).

1 Corinthians 16:13 Be on your guard; stand firm in the faith; be men of courage; be strong. Do everything in love (NIV).

1 Corinthians 15:58 Therefore, my dear brothers, stand firm. Let nothing move you. Always give yourselves fully to the work of the Lord, because you know that your labor in the Lord is not in vain.

Also See. **Matthew 10:16**

Day 11: Today's Prayer
Read Aloud

Christ Jesus, thank You for Your many blessings. Lord, You are our Warrior and are mighty in battle. **(Psalm 24: 8)** Lord, I decree and declare that I will face life with divine courage. Christ Jesus, I lay down every battle in my life at Your feet. I lay down the internal battles at the Cross of Jesus Christ. I will not be swayed to the right or to the left. Christ Jesus, help me to face life fearlessly yet with wisdom. I will take courage as I stand for the Gospel of Jesus Christ, telling of the Lord's goodness. Through the blood of Jesus, I command every spirit of fear that may try to operate in my mind, heart, spirit, and life to be broken in Christ Jesus' Name. I will stand and conquer all adversity though Christ Jesus. Lord, no matter what the day brings, I know You are with me. In Christ Jesus' Name I pray. Amen.

Day 11: Be Encouraged

When things happen that we don't understand—or sometimes if there is not a clear picture of what is coming next—fear tries to creep in. Fear is a spirit, and it's an evil one. Sometimes when we are afraid, we want courage over the particular thing we fear. But what about having courage over fear itself? Give fear no place in your life. God has given you everything you need not only to be victorious but to stare life in the face and say, "I won't be afraid." God said in **2 Chronicles 20:15, "For the battle is not yours, but God's"** (KJV). God wants you to know that He is right there with you in the middle of every battle. Christ Jesus wants to fight for you; let the Lord take up your case. Once we turn our battles over to God, we should leave them there. God wants you to have enough courage to trust Him with what seems to be undone in your life. As you wait on God, remain in a right standing with Him. Make an effort to keep a pure heart and clear mind. Worship God through the good and tough times.

Day 11: Today's Goal

The next time you feel fear, rebuke the spirit of fear in Jesus' Name. When life presents a circumstance that is beyond your control, be brave enough to share your heart with God at that moment and tell Him exactly what is going on. Christ Jesus is never too busy and is always looking forward to hearing from you.

Day 11: From Your Own Perspective

What does being brave mean to you?

_____
_____
_____
_____
_____

How have you exercised courage today?

_____
_____
_____
_____
_____

What battles do you need heaven to fight on your behalf?

_____
_____
_____
_____
_____

Day 11: Daily Journal

DAY 12: Give Thanks

Today's Confession
Read Aloud

I decree and declare that I will practice an attitude of gratitude. I am always appreciative and thankful.

Day 12: What It Means to Be and What Is

- Appreciate: 1. To recognize the quality, significance, or magnitude. 2. To be fully aware of; realize. 3. To be thankful.[43]

Day 12: Bread for the Soul

1 Thessalonians 5:16-18 Be joyful always; pray continually; give thanks in all circumstances, for this is Gods will for you in Christ Jesus (NIV).

Psalm 100:4–5 Enter his gates with thanksgiving and his courts with praise; give thanks to him and praise his name. For the Lord is good and his love endures forever; his faithfulness continues through all generations (NIV).

Psalm 30:11–12 You turned my wailing into dancing; you removed my sackcloth and clothed me with joy, that my heart may sing to you and not be silent. O Lord my God, I will give you thanks forever (NIV).

Psalm 119:62 At midnight I rise to give you thanks for your righteous laws (NIV).

Psalm 140:13 Surely the righteous shall give thanks unto thy name: the upright shall dwell in thy presence (KJV).

Psalm 92:1 It is a good thing to give thanks unto the Lord, and to sing praises unto thy name, O Most High (KJV).

Psalm 107:1 O give thanks unto the Lord, for he is good: for his mercy endureth forever (KJV).

Psalm 136:1–3 Give thanks to the Lord, for he is good. His love endures forever. Give thanks to the God of gods. His love endures forever. Give thanks to the Lord of lords: his love endures forever (NIV).

Day 12: Today's Prayer
Read Aloud

Christ Jesus, I will enter Your gates with thanksgiving and Your courts with praise. Lord, I thank You for breathing life into my soul and body. Thank You, Father, for perfect health. I thank You, Christ, for the blessings of Your kingdom that You have lavished on me. Eternal God, thank You for being good to all humanity and making a place at Abraham's feast for all who accept Your Son Jesus. What is man that You are mindful of him **(Psalms 8:4)**? Yet Your favor rests on humanity. **(Luke 2:14)** Thank You, Christ Jesus, for Your endless love. Show me, Lord, how to show appreciation to my parents and to all in authority over me. Lord, grant me the grace to always remain thankful.

Transform my heart, Jesus, to be in a state of gratefulness. In Christ Jesus' Name I pray. Amen.

Day 12: Be Encouraged

As human beings, we often tend to look at what is not rather than at what is. Gratitude is a door to more. It's in the little things, such as when Mom drops you off at practice. Instead of just saying good-bye or turning to get out of the car, say, "Thanks for dropping me off, Mom." When Dad stays up an extra fifteen minutes to iron your clothes or to make your lunch for school the next morning, stop to say, "Dad, I appreciate you making my lunch." Every person, no matter how old or young, wants to feel appreciated, just as you do when you perform well on that test or clean your room. You don't want anyone to take your effort for granted.

Let Mom know that you don't take for granted that she washes, folds, and puts away your clothes. As a human, carry an attitude of gratitude, never entitlement, when people do things for you. When you are believing God for something, no matter how long the answer may seem to take, always give thanks for what you do have. No matter what answer you receive, give God thanks that His will in every situation is what will come to pass. There is always something to be thankful for. Thank God for life in your body, for the fact that you can walk on your own, for eyesight and for breath.

God wants to feel appreciated for what He has done. In the Bible when the Israelites were in the desert after being freed from Egypt, God sent down manna from heaven for them to eat. Instead of being thankful that the Almighty God sent down food, they complained because it wasn't what they wanted to eat. That particular story didn't end well for some of the Israelites **(Numbers 11)**. Complaining is the fastest way to shut the door to the overflow of blessings. Showing gratitude to God and giving thanks as if you had all you ever wanted opens the door for blessings to come your way. Show God that He is more than enough for you. If things do not come as fast as you wish, give God praise simply because He is God.

Day 12: Today's Goal

Tell three people "thank-you" today. You can thank the person in front of you for holding the door open. Or even thank your little brother for setting your place at the table (even if it was his chore). Repeat this for the next three days.

Day 12: From Your Own Perspective

What are ten things you can thank God for right now?

_____
_____
_____
_____

How can you show your parents that you appreciate them? For example, what about writing them a letter or making them an appreciation gift? For example a card.

_____
_____
_____
_____

What would you like to be appreciated for?

_____
_____
_____
_____

Day 12: Daily Journal

DAY 13: Friends

Today's Confession
Read Aloud

I decree and declare that I make friends easily. I am confident and outgoing. I am a fun, friendly, and wise person. I am a positive influence on those around me.

Day 13: What It Means to Be and What Is

- Friend: A person one knows, likes, and trusts.[44]

- Friendly: 1a. Characteristic of or behaving like a friend. b. Outgoing and pleasant in social relations.[45]

Day 13: Bread for the Soul

Proverbs 18:24 A man that hath friends must shew himself friendly: and there is a friend that sticketh closer than a brother (KJV).

Luke 6:31 Do unto others as you would have them do to you (NIV).

Proverbs 22:24–25 Do not make friends with a hot-tempered man; do not associate with one easily angered, or you may learn his ways and get yourself ensnared (NIV).

Romans 12:18 If it is possible, as far as it depends on you, live at peace with everyone (NIV).

1 Corinthians 15:33 Do not be misled: "Bad company corrupts good character" (NIV).

Psalms 119:63 I am a friend to all who fear you, to all who follow your precepts (NIV).

Matthew 7:12 So in everything, do to others what you would have them do to you, for this sums up the Law and the Prophets.

Day 13: Today's Prayer
Read Aloud

Christ Jesus, I thank You for Your love. Christ Jesus, You are a friend like no other, the friend who sticks closer than a brother. (**Proverbs 18:24**) I thank You, Father, for placing genuine and loyal friends around me. I decree and declare that friends who have divine assignment in my life will be drawn to me. I thank You, Lord, for friends who serve Jesus Christ. Lord, let me forever influence those around me in a positive ways, and I pray they will do the same for me. Lord please tear down every friendship that the kingdom of darkness will try to use as a distraction or snare in my life. Jesus please tear down every negative association in my life. Holy Spirit, I pray that You will screen every person who walks into my life. God, I pray that Your right hand will sweep through my sphere of influence both in the natural and in the spiritual. Jesus, remove the hidden agenda of the kingdom of darkness from around me and replace it with Your good pleasures. Help me to be the type of friend who is pleasing to You. I decree and declare that I am a light for You, Christ Jesus. I thank You, Christ Jesus, that I have a great personality. Help me to be an engaging person. I pray, Father, that You will open the windows of heaven; bless my life. Help me to be more outgoing and confident. In Christ Jesus' Name I pray. Amen.

Day 13: Be Encouraged

God wants you to have friendships here in the earthly realm. As humans, we were made to have fellowship. God desires that you allow Him to help you choose the right friends. God wants people in your life who actually have a purpose for being there. One friend may be there to cheer you up when you are down; another friend may be there for more serious matters, such as helping you in this Christian walk. Treat people with kindness. Treat others how you want to be treated even if they are not your closest friends.

Some people will come into your life for a lifetime; others only for a season. Never give seasonal people lifetime responsibilities. God desires for you to have friends who are a good influence in all areas. As a young person, you will meet many different people. Know that you are a treasure, and people are blessed to have you in their life. You don't ever have to try to make someone be your friend or go out of your way to fit into what someone else wants you to be. If you have to step outside of your true self or out of who God says you are to be someone's friend, that person shouldn't be in your space.

You are a rare jewel; know it, believe it, and accept it. Sometimes diamonds and other rare jewels are found deep in the earth. They may be covered with rocks or mud. Someone had to dig to find that treasure. Real friends take the time to get to know the real you. Make room for people who sought you as a friend even on days when you may not have been at your best. A friend loves at all times. **(Proverbs 17:17)** Not just when someone fits a particular mold. Make friends at the Holy Spirit's discretion. You are a child of the Most High God.

God wants you to know that He is the greatest friend you will ever have. Christ Jesus chose you as a friend a long time ago; receive His gift of friendship. Ask Christ Jesus how He is doing and if there is anything you can do for Him. Be the type of friend to God who inquires of His heart and not one who speaks to Him only to make requests. Christ Jesus searches the earth for those who will seek Him. Just as we look forward to speaking to our friends or hanging out with them, God looks forward to hearing from you every single day.

Day 13: Today's Goal

Today, speak to someone you don't normally converse with. It doesn't have to be anything drawn out. Just say hello. You will be surprised at what can unfold when you step outside of your comfort zone. Make friends based on what suits you, not based on the "in" crowd. And remember, smiles are contagious, so share one today.

Day 13: From Your Own Perspective

How can you influence your friends in a positive way?

_____
_____
_____
_____

What characteristics do you want your friends to have?

_____
_____
_____
_____

How do you intend to be a good friend?

_____
_____
_____
_____
_____

Day 13: Daily Journal

DAY 14: Humility

Today's Confession
Read Aloud

I decree and declare that I am humble in spirit, my attitude, and my actions. I will seek to exalt Christ Jesus at all times.

Day 14: What It Means to Be and What Is

- Humble: 1. Meek or modest. 2. Deferentially respectful.[46]

Day 14: Bread for the Soul

James 4:10 Humble yourselves before the Lord, and he will lift you up (NIV).

Matthew 18:4 Therefore whoever humbles himself like this child is greatest in the kingdom of heaven (NIV).

Matthew 23:12 For whoever exalts himself will be humbled, and whoever humbles himself will be exalted (NIV).

Matthew 20:26-28 But it shall not be so among you: but whosoever will be great among you, let him be your minister; And whosoever will be chief among you, let him be your servant: even as the Son of man came not to be ministered unto, but to minster, and to give his life as a ransom for many (KJV).

Day 14: Today's Prayer
Read Aloud

Lord, I thank You for this day. Christ Jesus, in all Your majesty, You are still humble. You submit Yourself to God the Father in all things. You came to earth to serve Your children by ministering to our souls. I pray, Father, that You will help me to remain humble in my walk with You and in my everyday life. Lord, I decree and declare that I will give all glory to Your Name instead of seeking glory for myself. Christ Jesus, help me to humble myself like a little child in spirit that I may truly receive the kingdom of the Living God. Christ Jesus, today I humble myself to You as a servant. I set my agenda aside and take up the cause of the Lord Jesus Christ. In my humbleness, Jesus, I will lift up Your Name. I will tell of Your wonders and of the graces that are embedded in Your love. I abase myself before You, Lord. I decree and declare I am modest, and joyfully so. In Christ Jesus' Name I pray. Amen.

Day 14: Be Encouraged

The easiest way to remain humble is to seek to bring glory to Christ Jesus rather than to yourself. Whether in sports, class, or just everyday life, seek to honor God first. God honors those who honor Him. As you read in the scripture, those who seek to exalt themselves are humbled. Sometimes even in a disagreement in which you know without a shadow of a doubt you are right, you can humble yourself—not by changing your opinion but simply by making peace.

Everyone has to learn at some point to let God decide when to put them on display. There is nothing wrong with being proud of yourself or sharing your accomplishments with others. But as you do great things, always remember to encourage others, even in simple tasks. If you got an A on your history test and your friend got a C, don't just show your grade. Offer to help out that friend for the next test, or simply say, "Good job." We all have to make the choice to glorify God over ourselves. Humility shines a light that pride simply does not.

Day 14: Today's Goal

When something good happens to you today or when you accomplish something, take a moment and tell God thank you. Even if you have a chance to share what you did with others, tell how God graced and helped you in that task.

Day 14: From Your Own Perspective

How can you be more humble as a person?

_____
_____
_____

How will you give God glory today for what you accomplished?

_____
_____
_____

Day 14: Daily Journal

DAY 15: Designed to Rule

Today's Confession
Read Aloud

I decree and declare that I am walking in divine rulership granted by the Living God. Christ Jesus has granted me citizenship in the Kingdom of the Eternal God.

Day 15: What It Means to Be and What Is

- Ruler: One who rules or governs.[47]

- Ruling: Exercising control or authority.[48]

Day 15: Bread for the Soul

Romans 8:16–17 The Spirit himself testifies with our spirit that we are God's children. Now if we are children, then we are heirs—heirs of God and coheirs with Christ, if indeed we share in his sufferings in order that we may also share in his glory (NIV).

Genesis 1:26 Then God said, "Let us make man in our image, in our likeness, and let them rule over the fish of the sea and the birds of the air, over the livestock, over all the earth, and over all the creatures that move along the ground" (NIV).

Day 15: Today's Prayer
Read Aloud

Christ Jesus, You are King of kings and Lord of lords. All power in heaven and in earth has been given to You. **(Matthew 28:18)** Lord, I pray that You will show me, as a child of the King, how to rule well. Christ Jesus, help me govern my life and earthly affairs as You govern things of the entire universe—with justice. Lord, let Your will be done on earth as it is in heaven, through me. **(Matthew 6:10)** Lord, teach me the ways of Your government, which is not of this world. Jesus, teach me the protocols of the courts of heaven. Teach me how to administer justice. Through the blood of Jesus, I command every hindrance in the spirit realm to tremble and release the what God has granted me through grace. May those hindrances be no more. God, You are a consuming fire. **(Matthew 12:29)** Lord, let the enemy's plans for my life be consumed by Your fire this day. I decree and declare that not even the dust of the enemy's barracks will remain around my life. I decree and declare that I shall live as royalty, in spirit. I will begin to understand and value the things of the kingdom of God above all things in this world. Christ Jesus, may You grant me a place with those who minister before Your royal court. Minister to me, Lord, about the architecture of Your kingdom and what every facet of it represents. In Christ Jesus' Name I pray. Amen.

Day 15: Be Encouraged

You are royalty. God gave man dominion in the beginning, and rulership is a very serious responsibility. When you rule, someone is always watching you, and you have the power to affect things around you. Divine rulership is something that is learned and matured over time. It's learned through the Spirit of Christ Jesus and the Word of God. You are a ruler over everything you have control over; your attitude, associations, words, bedroom, school, and everyday decisions. Make the decision not just to be a ruler but to walk in divine rulership. Divine rulership has everything to do with making divine decisions. Divine decisions positively affect the world around you as well as your spirit. Divine decisions are engraved on the path of righteousness. The bible says in **Psalms 37:23**, **"The steps of a good man are ordered by the Lord: and he delighteth in his way" (KJV)**. Allow God to give you a vision of the long-term effects of your everyday decisions. You are faced with temporary decisions every single day, such as what shoes you will wear. Then there are the permanent decisions, such as who you will serve. Never make a permanent decision based on a temporary situation. Our struggles in this life that seem so hard are temporary; there is a promise beyond this world. That is eternal life. The bible says in **Romans 8:18**, **"I consider that our present sufferings are not worth comparing with the glory that will be revealed in us" (NIV)**. Sometimes when people are hurt or angry, they make decisions based on how they feel at the time rather than on God's promises. The next time life gets rough, instead of making a decision based on a negative emotion, make one based on the promises of God. For instance, He says in **Hebrews 13:5, "Never will I leave you; never will I forsake you."** That is a promise from God. God wants you to rule well.

Day 15: Today's Goal

Make a choice to rule your day by the Spirit of the Living God. Look for God in all you do. In every decision you make today, be aware of God's presence in your life.

Day 15: From Your Own Perspective

What is one of the most important characteristics of a ruler?

_____
_____
_____
_____

What areas in your life do you rule well? Do you rule your studies, relationships, or even the upkeep of your room well?

_____
_____
_____
_____

Are there any areas in your life you need to start ruling according to God's standards?

_____
_____
_____
_____

Day 15: Daily Journal

DAY 16: Forgiveness

Today's Confession
Read Aloud

I decree and declare that I practice justice with all those around me. I am forgiving, merciful, and gracious.

Day 16: What It Means to Be and What Is

- Justice: 1. The quality of being just; fairness. 2. The principle or moral rightness; equity. 3. The upholding of what is just, fair treatment and due reward in accordance with honor, standards, or law.[49]

- Forgive: 1. To excuse for a fault or offense; pardon. 2. To stop feeling anger or resentment against. 3. To absolve from payment.[50]

- Mercy: 1. Compassionate treatment, especially of those under one's power. 3. A blessing.[51]

- Gracious: 1. Marked by kindness and warm courtesy.[52]

Day 16: Bread for the Soul

Proverbs 29:2 When the righteous are in authority, the people rejoice: but when the wicked beareth rule, the people mourn (KJV).

Matthew 18:21-22 Then Peter came to Jesus and asked, "Lord, how many times must I forgive my brother when he sins against me? Up to seven times?" Jesus answered, "I tell you, not seven times, but seventy-seven times" (NIV).

Matthew 6:12 Forgive us our debts, as we also have forgiven our debtors (NIV).

Matthew 6:14-15 For if you forgive men when they sin against you, your heavenly Father will also forgive you. But if you do not forgive men their sins, your heavenly Father will not forgive you your sins (NIV).

Matthew 5:7 Blessed are the merciful for they will be shown mercy (NIV).

Mark 12:30-31 Love the Lord your God with all your heart and all your soul and with all your mind and with all your strength. The second is this: Love your neighbor as yourself. There is no commandment greater than these.

Day 16: Today's Prayer
Read Aloud

Christ Jesus, thank You for Your grace and love. Jesus, I pray that You will give me the heart, will, and desire to forgive. No matter what people's sins are against me, I will forgive them from the deepest places in me. Lord, You have commanded us to release others from their wrongs against us. So today, Christ Jesus, I release every person who has offended me from my birth until now. Lord, I decree and declare that I am free. I let go of the pain and disappointment. Through the blood of Jesus I come against every bitter and unforgiving spirit. Those things will not dwell inside of me. I tear down every stronghold of hate in Jesus' Name. Lord, You forgave me for a lifetime of sins, so I will hold no one hostage for a season of indiscretions. I forgive them, Lord; I let them go. Let forgiveness become my lifestyle every day. I command every weight to drop off my heart in Jesus' Name. And I pray that the Holy Spirit will uproot every thought of revenge in my mind. May those things be consumed by the fire of the Holy Ghost. Teach me to love the way You do, Christ Jesus. Holy Spirit, shield my heart from the spirit of unforgiveness. Take the yoke from around my neck. Help me to lead those who have offended me to You, Christ Jesus, that they may know of Your love. Lord, I decree and declare this day that my offenders are not guilty, just as You did for me. In Christ Jesus' Name I pray. Amen.

Day 16: Be Encouraged

God commands us to forgive. Forgiveness is an act that comes from within. Its takes grace from God to truly forgive, because forgiveness is a manifestation of the Spirit of God. God requires us to forgive people regardless of the situation. Forgiveness is something that can happen in a moment, but sometimes it happens over time. The greatest example of forgiveness is Jesus Christ, who died on the cross for our sins.

With forgiveness comes wisdom. If someone purposely keeps hurting you or trying to take advantage of your good nature, ask God whether that particular individual should still be in your life. It's possible to forgive someone and move on with your day or even your life.

If you are in a situation you may not know how to deal with it. Ask the Holy Spirit to come to your defense. No matter how badly it hurts, always seek to forgive to keep your internal state clear. Forgiveness is not for the person who offended you but rather for you. Forgiveness gives you peace and keeps you in right standing with God. Don't feel guilty if the anger or resentment doesn't all go away in the next hour or even month. God understands and wants to help you get over those hurdles one day at a time.

Forgiveness is part of walking in love. Its takes a lifetime to learn what it truly means to walk in love. It takes more than a lifetime to know just how far forgiveness can go; God's love for us stretches all the way into eternity.

No matter what you may have a guard up against at this time, always keep your heart open to Christ Jesus. See God for who He is, not through the mistakes of those around us. God can see our pain even when we are only crying inside. When you forgive, don't be afraid to release the pain of that person's offense to God. He is there to love you back to the place of healing and being completely whole. God is just, and He expects us to also practice justice. Grace, mercy, and forgiveness are all part of the justice system in the kingdom of God. If you are ever faced with a situation and don't see how you could ever let a particular offense go, just pray, "Christ, teach me and grant me the grace to forgive again."

Day 16: Today's Goal

Make it a point today to forgive someone who may have hurt you. You may decide to talk with that individual and tell them you forgive them. You may not be around the person to tell them that, but you can tell Christ Jesus,

"Lord, I release (**person's name who offended you**) and their offense against me into Your hands."

Day 16: From Your Own Perspective

Is there someone you may have wronged and need to ask for their forgiveness?

_____
_____
_____
_____

Is there anyone you need to forgive?

_____
_____
_____
_____

Are you believing Christ Jesus to repair a broken friendship or relationship in your life?

_____
_____
_____
_____

Day 16: Daily Journal

DAY 17: I'm Better

Today's Confession
Read Aloud

I decree and declare that I am always improving, both in my walk with Christ Jesus and in the natural realm. I am always getting better. My spirit will flourish in the Kingdom of the Living God.

Day 17: Bread for the Soul

Philippians 1:6 Being confident of this, that he who began a good work in you will carry it on to completion until the day of Christ Jesus (NIV).

Hebrews 13:20–21 May the God of peace, who through the blood of the eternal covenant brought back from the dead our Lord Jesus, that great Shepherd of the sheep, equip you with everything good for doing his will, and may he work in us what is pleasing to him, through Jesus Christ, to whom be glory for ever and ever. Amen (NIV).

2 Corinthians 12:9–10 But he said to me, "My grace is sufficient for you, for my power is made perfect in weakness." Therefore I will boast more gladly about my weaknesses, so that Christ's power may rest on me. That is why, for Christ's sake, I delight in weaknesses, in insults, in hardships, in persecutions, in difficulties. For when I am weak, then I am strong (NIV).

Day 17: Today's Prayer
Read Aloud

Christ Jesus, thank You for loving me. Lord, I give You everything that I see as an imperfection along with what I see as perfections. I pray that those imperfections will be the perfect tools to bring glory to Your Name. Christ Jesus, Your strength is made perfect in weaknesses. So from this day forward, I will no longer see weakness but God's strength in me. I decree and declare that I will improve academically, spiritually, socially, and physically through the power of Holy Spirit. Jesus I pray to grow closer to You and fall more in in love with You every day. Lord, show me Your plan in all things. I will choose to have faith over every aspect of my life. You make all things new Father. So take everything I have and turn into a beautiful masterpiece, that displays Your glory. In Christ Jesus' Name I pray. Amen.

Day 17: Be Encouraged

We are all made of flesh, which means we are born into sin. There is a myth that Christians have to be perfect; that simply is not true. Jesus came to die on the cross because He knew we as humans are not perfect. God does expect us to be consistent in our walk with Him. God knows whether an individual is living a rebellious lifestyle or has simply fallen short. This life is one of fighting through and mastering sin. **Genesis 4:7** says, referring to sin, that it desires to have you, but you must master it. God said in His word that all sins would be forgiven **(See. Matthew 12:31)**. Of course, we must know that forgiveness relates to repentance, and repentance entails turning away from sin, but there is no sin that is too bad to be forgiven. Think of it this way: Christ Jesus knew all the sins you would commit, but He still died for you. God still chose you for His kingdom, and He loved each one of us while we were yet sinners. **Romans 5:8** says, **"But God demonstrates his own love for us in this: While we were still sinners, Christ died for us."**

That mind-set of needing to be perfect affects every area of people's lives, and not always in a good way. Whether in daily tasks or accomplishments, God is pleased with your best—with straight A's or C's. Whether you are a size 2 or 22, God loves you right where you are. If good characteristics in you may not be perfected at this time, it does not mean God is not with you or pleased with you. The Word says that God will complete His work in you.

God wants to work with you day in and day out. We are all in process no matter how long we have been saved or have known of God. Everyone in God's kingdom is in the process of becoming one of the sons of God. The Bible says in **Romans 8:19 The creation waits in eager expectation for the sons of God to be revealed (NIV)**. God is still working on you, and in due season He will reveal just who you are in Him. You don't have to be, pray, or sound like anyone else. This is *your* walk with God. Enjoy it! Let God's light shine through you as He sees fit.

Day 17: Today's Goal

Look deep within yourself. Pick out an area you want God to touch in your life. This is between you and God. Let the Lord do a new thing in you.

Day 17: From Your Own Perspective

What are three areas you want the Lord to perfect in your life?

_____
_____
_____
_____
_____

What are you willing to do to improve in these areas?

_____
_____
_____
_____
_____

Day 17: Daily Journal

DAY 18: Keep Going!

Today's Confession
Read Aloud

I decree and declare that I will endure in the ways of Christ Jesus until the end. I will never give up. I will never quit. I am a champion.

Day 18: What It Means to Be and What Is

- Endure: 1. To carry on, despite hardships; undergo. 2. To continue in existence; last.[53]

- Champion: One who holds first place or wins first place in a contest.[54]

Day 18: Bread for the Soul

Romans 8:37 No, in all these things, we are more than conquerors through him who loved us (NIV).

Philippians 3:14 I press on toward the goal to win the prize for which God has called me heavenward in Christ Jesus (NIV).

Hebrews 12:1–3 Therefore, since we are surrounded by such a great cloud of witnesses, let us throw off everything that hinders and the sin that so easily entangles, and let us run with perseverance the race marked out for us. Let us fix our eyes on Jesus, the author and perfecter of our faith, who for the joy set before him endured the cross, scorning its shame, and sat down at the right hand of the throne of God. Consider him who endured such opposition from sinful men, so that you will not grow weary and lose heart (NIV).

Romans 5:1–5 Therefore, since we have been justified through faith, we have peace with God through our Lord Jesus Christ, through whom we have gained access by faith into this grace in which we now stand. And we rejoice in the hope of the glory of God. Not only so, but we also rejoice in our sufferings, because we know that suffering produces perseverance; perseverance, character; and character hope. And hope does not disappoint us because God has poured out his love into our hearts by the Holy Spirit, whom he has given us (NIV).

Matthew 24:13 But he that shall endure unto the end, the same will be saved (KJV).

Matthew 24:13 But he who stands firm to the end will be saved (NIV).

Psalm 26:3 For your love is ever before me, and I walk continually in your truth (NIV).

James 5:11 Behold, we count them happy which endure (KJV).

Day 18: Today's Prayer
Read Aloud

Christ Jesus, thank You for the strength You have given me to win. Your divine power has given me everything I need for life, Lord. **(2 Peter 1:3)** Christ Jesus, help me to conquer this life through Your blood. Lord, let a fire that burns for You; one that cannot be quenched be embedded in my soul and heart through Your precious Holy Spirit. Christ Jesus, I pray for the desire to know You more, to serve You, to please You, and to do Your will. I pray, Father, that my spiritual well-being will mean more than anything else. Lord, Your Word says in **Ecclesiastes 9:11, The race is not given to the swift or the strong (NIV)**. I know victory comes to those who endure until the end. Christ Jesus, help me to endure; push me, Lord, to keep going. I decree and declare that I will not give up on You, Christ Jesus, or on myself. I accept that You are waiting for me at the finish line. I know You are with me every step of the way. Christ Jesus, thank You for wanting the very best for me; I know that Your promises are yes and amen **(2 Corinthians 1:20)**. Help me to press on, Father, to a place of promise. Christ Jesus, in all things, in You I will find peace. Christ Jesus, I pray that Your right hand will continue to crush the kingdom of darkness and everything that tries to hinder me from making it to You. In Christ Jesus' Name I pray. Amen.

Day 18: Be Encouraged

To endure takes strength, and strength is built by perseverance. Most times perseverance springs forth when we are in a tough situation. God wants you to know that He understands the times we are living in. God knew what would be necessary for us to cross the finish line into an eternity with Him: *Grace!* The Bible says in **2 Corinthians 12:9,** But he said to me, "My grace is sufficient for you, for my power is made perfect in weakness (NIV)."

It also says in **1 Corinthians 10:13** No temptation has seized you except what is common to man. And God is faithful; he will not let you be tempted beyond what you can bear. But when you are tempted, he will also provide a way out so that you can stand up under it (NIV).

No matter what the temptation or trial you may face, God has already given you the grace to be victorious. There is a way of escape. God wants you to know that the strength you are looking for is in Him. God is cheering for you and is delighted to see you pressing on even through the most trying circumstances. God believes in you, and He always will.

People often look outside for the answers when the true answer is within. Jesus said in **Luke 17:21, "The kingdom of God is within you."** God wants you to keep going. Don't quit! In the moments when heaven seems silent, know that God is always there. God gives us the opportunities in this life to use the spiritual training given to us through His Word and by spending time with Him to graduate to the next level. God loves to see His children fight the good fight of faith. **(1 Timothy 6:12)**

God responds to faith. He loves when we choose to live for Him beyond what we see or feel. Even when life seems to get the best of us, God is looking forward to the day we pick ourselves up, dust ourselves off, and get back in there. This Christian walk is a faith walk. We have to believe that every single day we wake up, God has breathed grace into our lungs; we have another day to get it right. Walk with God based on trust in Him alone. Don't put your trust in what you see, in this world, or in temporary luxuries. There are greater things to obtain, and they are in Christ Jesus. Every believer who crosses the finish line holds first place.

Day 18: Today's Goal

When you are ready, make the decision to win. Before you take on any task today, tell yourself, "I am a champion."

Day 18: From Your Own Perspective

What do you look forward to when you wake up every day?

_____
_____
_____
_____

What are your long-term goals?

_____
_____
_____
_____

What does the heart of every champion carry?

_____
_____
_____
_____

Day 18: Daily Journal

DAY 19: Truthful

Today's Confession
Read Aloud

I decree and declare that I am trustworthy, honest, and a person of integrity.

Day 19: What It Means to Be and What Is

- Trustworthy: Warranting trust; reliable.[55]

- Honest: Not deceptive or fraudulent; genuine. 3a. True; not false.[56]

- Integrity: Steadfast adherence to a strict moral or ethical code. 2. Soundness 3. Completeness; unity.[57]

Day 19: Bread for the Soul

Proverbs 12:22 The Lord detests lying lips, but he delights in men who are truthful (NIV).

Proverbs 20:7 The just man walketh in his integrity: his children are blessed after him (KJV).

Psalms 41:12 In my integrity you uphold me and set me in your presence forever (NIV).

Psalm 25:21 May integrity and uprightness protect me, because my hope is in you (NIV).

Psalm 26:11 But as for me, I will walk in mine integrity: redeem me, and be merciful unto me (KJV).

Proverbs 6:16–19 There are six things the Lord hates, seven that are detestable to him: haughty eyes, a lying tongue, hands that shed innocent blood, a heart that devises wicked schemes, feet that are quick to rush to evil, a false witness who pours out lies, and a man who stirs up dissension among brothers (NIV).

Day 19: Today's Prayer
Read Aloud

God, I thank You for another day to seek You. Lord God, You have commanded us to be holy as You are holy. I pray, Father, that You will always give me the courage to be honest and accountable. Lord, help me to be truthful with myself and with others. You delight in truth, Christ Jesus. You are the Living Word. I bind every spirit of deceitfulness in Jesus' Name. I decree and declare that regardless of the cost, I will put my trust in You, Lord. I decree and declare that I will never be swayed by the ambitions or incentives of people. Through the blood of Jesus, I pray that every entanglement of deceit be dismantled in my life and spirit. I will bask in the pleasure of Your Word, Father. Lord, You have given me the ability to speak; I give that ability back to You. I will speak well of others, and I will remain positive. Lord, guard my tongue, and help me to think before I speak. In Christ Jesus' Name I pray. Amen.

Day 19: Be Encouraged

God is a God of truth and light. Every day we are given the opportunity to be honest. It could be a small situation, such as your mom asking if you did all your homework. Some instances may be bigger. Most times we tell a lie to escape the consequences for an action already taken. Christ Jesus wants each of us to get in the habit of being honest. This is something required by the Living God, not just by those in authority over us. Lying seems easy, but it comes with a price. God detests lies. The next time you are given the opportunity to be honest, do so. You may be surprised at the response that you receive. If someone asks you a question and you know the response may hurt their feelings, it's OK to not to comment at all. Remember, honesty is a character trait God expects all of us to have.

Day 19: Today's Goal

Make it a point to be honest today.

Day 19: From Your Own Perspective

Is it possible to be polite and still be honest? Why or why not?

_____
_____
_____
_____
_____

What are some issues you want people to always be honest with you about?

_____
_____
_____
_____
_____

Do you extend to people the same courtesy of honesty that you expect to receive?

_____
_____
_____
_____
_____

Day 19: Daily Journal

DAY 20: Happiness

Today's Confession
Read Aloud

I decree and declare that I am happy and joyful. I always have a reason to smile. I have the peace of God, that surpasses all understanding.

Day 20: Bread for the Soul

Nehemiah 8:10 For the joy of the Lord is your strength (NIV).

Philippians 4:6–7 Do not be anxious for anything, but in everything, by prayer and petition, with thanksgiving, present your requests to God. And the peace of God, which transcends all understanding, will guard your hearts and minds in Christ Jesus (NIV).

Psalm 28:7–8 The Lord is my strength and my shield; my heart trusts in him, and I am helped. My heart leaps for joy, and I will give thanks to him in song. The Lord is the strength of his people, a fortress of salvation for his anointed one (NIV).

Psalm 144:15 Happy is that people, that is in such a case: yea, happy is that people whose God is the Lord (KJV).

Psalm 146:5 Happy is he that hath the God of Jacob for his help, whose hope is in the Lord his God (KJV).

Day 20: Today's Prayer
Read Aloud

Christ Jesus, I thank You for Your Joy. Lord, I just pray that You will help me to be truly happy inside. I pray that my happiness shall be steadfast in You. Lord, help me to see the beauty of Your holiness in everything around me. I open my spirit to receive the peace of God that surpasses all understanding. Christ Jesus, please uproot and take away every spirit of sadness in my life. Please give me inexpressible and glorious joy. **(1 Peter 1:8)** Holy Spirit please take control of my emotions and feelings. Christ Jesus, You are my light and the rock on which I stand. **(Matthew 7:24-25)** The source of my happiness will be in You. I thank You, Lord, for smiling down on me. Your face shines upon my spirit. Lord, give me divine laughter that overflows so that no matter what others around me may be going through, they will also have a reason to smile. Lord, I know that You want me to be happy, and there is always joy in Your will. Christ Jesus, I pray that my life will be the reason God smiles and that I will be a vessel that makes heaven happy. In Christ Jesus' Name I pray. Amen.

Day 20: Be Encouraged

Happiness is an internal state of being. You could say that happiness is a state of mind or even a choice. True happiness comes from the heart of God. Happiness is a gift from God that manifests peace; thus, it's easy for happiness to dwell within a person in whom God dwells.

An important aspect of happiness is the source of that happiness. Some people appear to have nothing going for themselves, yet they are happier than those who seem to have the world laid at their feet. If the source of a person's happiness is temporary, so will be their happiness. But if the source is eternal, then that happiness will also be eternal. God is the Alpha and Omega; He always has been, always is, and forever will be.

We all get sad or down sometimes; it's called emotion. But regardless of how down you get, there is a power in you that is greater than the power in the world. That power is Jesus Christ **(1 John 4:4)**. Christ Jesus is that spark you need to get going; He is the light the shines in the darkest hour. God genuinely wants you to be happy not just for a little while but always. Even in trials, let God's joy be your joy. Sometimes our joy in the middle of sorrow is worship to God, even with tears in our eyes. Christ Jesus pleased God very much when He was crucified on the cross, even though the experience was painful for Him. The fact that it was God's will for Him to endure the cross was enough for Jesus to keep going.

One thing about God is that when we endure trials for the sake of His glory, He always restores us. Strive to make God happy first, yourself, and then others.

Isaiah 53:10–11 says this: "Yet it was the Lord's will to crush him and cause him to suffer, and though the Lord makes his life a guilt offering, he will see his offspring and prolong his days, and the will of the Lord will prosper in his hand. After the suffering of his soul, he will see the light of life, and be satisfied, by his knowledge my righteous servant will justify many, and he will bear their iniquities (NIV)."

Day 20: Today's Goal

Identify something that makes you happy that isn't materialistic. Are you happy when you use your gift—for example, dancing, singing, playing a sport, or writing? Are you happy when you get to view nature? Identify that place of happiness, and try to visit that place once per day.

Day 20: From Your Own Perspective

Do other people have the right to decide if you are happy?

_____
_____
_____
_____
_____

What does happiness mean to you? What is the foundation of your happiness built on?

_____
_____
_____
_____
_____

What have you done to brighten someone else's day?

_____
_____
_____
_____
_____

Day 20: Daily Journal

DAY 21: Complete

Today's Confession
Read Aloud

I decree and declare that I am whole. No good thing is lacking in my life.

Day 21: Bread for the Soul

Psalm 111:1 Praise ye the Lord. I will praise the Lord with my whole heart, in the assembly of the upright, and in the congregation (KJV).

Psalm 119:33–35 Teach me, O Lord, to follow your decree; then I will keep them to the end. Give me understanding, and I will keep your law and obey it with all my heart. Direct me in the path of your commands, for there I find delight (NIV).

Jeremiah 24:7 And I will give them a heart to know me, that I am the Lord. They shall be my people, and I will be their God, for they shall return to me with their whole heart (NIV).

Matthew 9:22 But Jesus turned him about, and when he saw her, he said, "Daughter, be of good comfort; thy faith hath made thee whole." And the woman was made whole from that hour (KJV).

Day 21: Today's Prayer
Read Aloud

Christ Jesus, I thank You that there is no lack in my life. I thank You that, as it says in Psalms 84:11, "no good thing will You withhold from me as I walk blamelessly before You." I do not lack physically, spiritually, emotionally, mentally, or financially. Christ Jesus, I pray that in all these areas, You will make me whole. I decree and declare that my heart is intact and remains in Your hand. In the Name of Jesus Christ, I command the spirit of lack to be destroyed and uprooted in my life. I pray every generational stronghold that will try to manifest lack of any kind in my life is no more. Holy Spirit let every curse be broken and every chain removed, in the Name of Jesus. Christ Jesus, I decree and declare this day that lack is consumed by the Holy Ghost's fire, never to resurface again. Lord, give my spirit direction to the place where the bounty of Your kingdom dwells. Christ Jesus, I pray that You will open the storehouses of heaven and fill me until I overflow. I give You my whole heart, Christ Jesus. I am asking that You construct and orchestrate the manifestation of my destiny. I will always depend on You, Lord, to be my everything. In Christ Jesus' Name I pray. Amen.

Day 21: Be Encouraged

Being whole has everything to do with the foundation inside of you. God wants every area in your life to be full and abundant. The state of your heart is one of the most important things to God. Along with that is the well-being of your spirit. God is interested in filling you with His Spirit. Every time you read the Word of God, you are being filled. Whenever you spend time in the presence of God, you are being filled. Even when trials come, God is still filling you with strength. Trials increase your faith, and to be filled, you first have to be emptied. God wants to remove everything inside you that may be a stumbling block. God has to purify all of us daily; there isn't a perfect human being on this earth. Use every opportunity you have to fill yourself with more of God through what you see, hear, and say. Whatever you fill yourself with usually comes back out at some point. Make an effort to pour positive feed into your spirit, putting yourself on the path of being made whole. As God begins to deal with the inside of you, your outside world will comply.

Day 21: Today's Goal

Make a list of things you may need to delete from your life that may take away from your relationship with God. For example, certain music, T.V. shows, certain associations etc.

Day 21: From Your Own Perspective

What area in your life seems to be lacking right now?

_____
_____
_____
_____

Are there things that come out of you that you would like God to remove?

_____
_____
_____
_____

When good or bad things happen in life, where do you feel it the most? Is it your heart, mind, or maybe it is your emotions that are affected? What can you do to strengthen that particular area? God wants to be the caretaker of the most vulnerable places in us all.

_____
_____
_____
_____

Day 21: Daily Journal

DAY 22: Diligence

Today's Confession
Read Aloud

I decree and declare that I am faithful and diligent. I practice self-discipline in positive and righteous ways.

Day 22: What It Means to Be and What Is

- Faithful: Adhering firmly and devotedly; loyal.[58]

- Diligent: Marked by or done with persevering, painstaking effort or care.[59]

- Discipline: Training expected to produce a specific character or pattern of behavior.[60]

Day 22: Bread for the Soul

Proverbs 10:4 Lazy hands make a man poor, but diligent hands bring wealth (NIV).

Proverbs 13:4 The sluggard craves and gets nothing, but the desires of the diligent are fully satisfied (NIV).

2 Peter 3:13–14 Nevertheless we, according to his promise, look for new heavens and a new earth; wherein dwelleth righteousness. Wherefore, beloved, seeing that ye look for such things, be diligent, that ye may be found of him in peace, without spot and blameless (KJV).

1 Timothy 6:11–12 But thou, O man of God, flee these things, and follow after righteousness, godliness, faith, love, patience, meekness. Fight the good fight of faith, lay hold on eternal life, whereunto thou art also called, and hast professed a good profession before many witnesses (KJV).

Matthew 25:21 His master replied, "Well done, good and faithful servant! You have been faithful with a few things; I will put you in charge of many things. Come and share in your master's happiness" (NIV).

Day 22: Today's Prayer
Read Aloud

Christ Jesus, I thank You for being faithful even when we are not. **(2 Timothy 2:13)** Lord, I just pray that You will grant me a divine spirit of consistency. I will work to be diligent over my prayer life and time spent in Your Word. I will be diligent in taking the necessary steps to fulfill my destiny in Your kingdom. Lord, show me how to be diligent over what is before me. No gift You give is small; You are a big God, and You do all things well. **(Mark 7:37)** I will be diligent over my schoolwork. Lord, as You give me ideas and inventions, I will be diligent until I see the finished products. Christ Jesus, help me not to be distracted or worried. All things are in Your hands.

(John 3:35) I pray that heaven will give me instruction, and I will act on heaven's timetable. Lord, I pray that I will never go before You and instead You will always lead me. I believe, Father, that there is something greater ahead of me, something only Your mind could have thought of. So I thank You now, Father. No task You have given me is too hard or too far away; through Christ Jesus, I am well able. In Christ Jesus' Name I pray. Amen.

Day 22: Be Encouraged

Being faithful has everything to do with being consistent. God expects us to be faithful at all times. Faith is believing without seeing. Christ Jesus wants us to be faithful over our daily lives even when it seems we aren't seeing the benefits of it right away. The bible says in **Romans 12:1,** "Therefore, I urge you, brothers, in view of God's mercy, to offer your bodies as living sacrifices, holy and pleasing to God; this is your spiritual act of worship. (NIV)"

We owe God everything. Nothing we do for God is in vain. God takes notice of the things man overlooks, and He rewards us. Sometimes when we do the right thing, we want people to see, but what is important is that God sees. Live your life to get the attention of heaven. Live your life so that on the day Jesus returns, He will say to you, "Well done, good and faithful servant!" (Matthew 25:21) Keep working, Keep going! People strive to leave behind a legacy on earth, which is a good thing, but take that a little bit further. Live a life that will never be forgotten by the Savior of the world, Christ Jesus.

Being faithful entails hanging in there until you get it done, no matter how long it takes. God is by your side, and He wants you to know that He sees your effort. Start with the little things. Make a decision right now to do something today to make God proud. The bible says in **Psalms 53:2, "God looks down from heaven on the sons of men to see if there are any who understand, any who seek God (NIV)."** Seek God through the way you live. A faithful life to God puts an individual in a position to continually hear from God. Keep living a faithful life unto the Lord Jesus Christ. Continually live so heaven will mark your life and your faith as *"never to be forgotten."*

Day 22: Today's Goal

Do something today to make God happy. Maybe try again at the same task that seemed hard in the past. God doesn't want you to quit, because He would never quit on you. No matter if, it's your walk with God, or trying to do better in school. God would prefer you try 1,000 more times than to ever give up. *Try again*!

Day 22: From Your Own Perspective

How can you present your body to God as a living sacrifice?

_____
_____
_____
_____

Do we have to be faithful in all things or just some things?

_____
_____
_____
_____

Day 22: Daily Journal

DAY 23: More Than Enough

Today's Confession
Read Aloud

I decree and declare that I am prosperous and opulent. I am spiritually prosperous in Christ Jesus.

Day 23: What It Means to Be and What Is

- Prosperous: 1. Successful. 2. Well-to-do; well-off.[61]

- Opulent: Possessing great wealth.[62]

Day 23: Bread for the Soul

3 John 2 Beloved, I wish above all things that thou mayest prosper and be in health, even as thy soul prospereth (KJV).

1 Chronicles 4:10 Jabez cried out to the God of Israel, "Oh that you would bless me and enlarge my territory! Let your hand be with me, and keep me from harm so that I may be free from pain." And God granted his request (NIV).

Matthew 6:19–21 Do not store up for yourselves treasures on earth, where moth and rust destroy, and where thieves break in and steal. But store up for yourselves treasures in heaven, where moth and rust do not destroy, and where thieves do not break in and steal. For where your treasure is, there your heart will be also (NIV).

Philippians 4:19 And my God will meet all your needs according to his glorious riches in Christ Jesus (NIV).

Day 23: Today's Prayer
Read Aloud

Christ Jesus, I thank You for the riches of Your love. Lord, give me an understanding of wealth beyond this world. Show me how to store up treasures for myself in heaven where thieves do not break in and steal. Lord, Your Word says that where my treasure is, my heart will be also. (Matthew 6:19–21) Christ Jesus, I pray that my treasure will be in You. I will serve You, God, because You are God, not for what I can obtain. Lord, let my heart be attached You, not to temporary things. Christ Jesus, teach me what prosperity means to You. Tell me all about the currency of heaven. Teach me, Lord, of Your wealth. No matter what I have in this life, I will use it to bring glory to Your Name. I decree and declare that I will not chase money; money will chase me. Divine opportunities and new ventures are chasing me down in Jesus' Name. I will walk in my purpose in the kingdom of God. I decree and declare opportunity, advancement, and promotion will come looking for me. I thank You, Lord, for delivering my mind and revealing to me a new thing. In Christ Jesus' Name I pray. Amen.

Day 23: Be Encouraged

Prosperity goes far beyond the earthly realm. Prosperity is a mental, spiritual, emotional, and physical state of being. Through the media, some commercial is always telling us what we need to have in order to feel prosperous. But can I tell you a secret; you were prosperous before the world began. When Jesus was on the earth, He didn't walk around looking like earthly kings, but He was and still is the Kings of kings. God desires for His children to seek Him for more than things that are created by man's hands. God wants you to seek Him for the type of prosperity that only He can give. There are greater things to obtain in this life than money, cars, homes, and so on. There is nothing wrong with having nice things, but don't let things define who you are. Don't ever see your relationship with God or God's love for you through materialistic and temporary possessions. Not everyone who has nice things is blessed by God. On the other hand, the fact that a person may not seem to have much does not mean God is not smiling down on them.

Don't ever think God doesn't want you to be successful. But is success that is limited to this world true success? In other words are you allowing God to use your accomplishments for His purposes? Don't limit God give Him everything you have. Christ Jesus longs for you to ask Him to bring you into your spiritual inheritance. That begins with accepting salvation through Christ Jesus. God wants to present a different perception to you of what prosperity is.

God is from everlasting to everlasting. (Isaiah 40:28, Psalms 103:17) So with all that humanity thinks it knows, we haven't even scratched the surface of God. Be an individual God can use to introduce something new to the world. Christ Jesus is always sharing things with those who are willing to receive and listen. True prosperity is never ending, which means your true prosperity is connected to and embedded in eternity with Christ Jesus.

Day 23: Today's Goal

Define prosperity in your own words, but don't use materialistic explanations in your definition. Some may find they have to really sit and think about this, but that is a good thing. That means you are in a place to receive that real definition of prosperity from Christ Jesus.

Day 23: From Your Own Perspective

What area in your spirit do you want God to prosper?

_____
_____
_____
_____

Can a person who has only the necessities of life be considered prosperous? Why or why not?

_____
_____
_____
_____

Day 23: Daily Journal

DAY 24: Healing

Today's Confession
Read Aloud

I decree and declare that I live in perfect physical, emotional, and mental health. I decree and declare that by Jesus stripes, I am healed. I have spiritual health through the blood of Christ Jesus and the Word of God.

Day 24: Bread for the Soul

Isaiah 53:4–5 Surely he took up our infirmities and carried our sorrows, yet we considered him stricken by God, smitten by him, and afflicted. But he was pierced for our transgressions, he was crushed for our iniquities; the punishment that brought us peace was upon him, and by his wounds we are healed (NIV).

Jeremiah 17:14 Heal me, O Lord, and I will be healed; save me and I will be saved, for you are the one I praise (NIV).

Exodus 15:26 For I am the Lord who heals you (NIV).

Hebrews 4:12-13 For the word of God is living and active. Sharper than any double-edged sword, it penetrates even to dividing soul and spirit, joints and marrow; it judges the thoughts and attitudes of the heart. Nothing in all creation is hidden from God's sight. Everything is uncovered and laid bare before the eyes of him to whom we must give account (NIV).

Day 24: Today's Prayer
Read Aloud

Christ Jesus, I thank You for Your healing power. Lord, You are Jehova-Ropheka, which means, "The Lord is healer." God, I pray that You heal my life as well as my spirit and body. Lord, I know that You have taken me unto Yourself. I speak to every blood cell, bone, joint, vein, artery, and brain function in my body and command each one to submit to the healing power that is in the Name of Jesus. I speak in the atmosphere and command the healing power of Jesus to come forth now. Lord, Jesus I pray that You will speak one word from on high that will change my entire life and existence. Your Word is sharper than any double-edged sword. **(Hebrews 4:12-13)** Christ Jesus, speak, and I will be made whole. I pray for Your grace and mercy. In Christ Jesus' Name I pray. Amen.

Day 24: Be Encouraged

Life sometimes throws things at us that seem unfair. Brokenness is not limited to bones; a person can have a broken heart. Broken hearts manifest out of broken situations. Christ Jesus wants you to know that no matter what area of your life may seem broken, you are healed. The things we sometimes face are meant to bring glory to God.

Look at the woman with the issue of blood **(See. Mark 5:25–34)** or the woman who washed Jesus' feet **(See. Luke 7:37–50)**. Both of these women believed in the midst of dire circumstances, and glory was brought to God because of it. Neither woman's story was ever forgotten. God wants you to know that you are not at a disadvantage. God uses the broken areas of our life to pour out His glory.

People's greatest anointing comes through their greatest test; look at Christ Jesus. People who have reason to seek God usually tap into a greater realm of faith than individuals who don't see a need. Sometimes the greater the need, the more we pursue God. The bible **says Hebrews 11:6, "And without faith it's impossible to please God, because anyone who comes to him must believe that he exists and that he rewards those who earnestly seek Him (NIV)."** We have to learn to thank God for our troubles because the trouble is what leads us to Him. We also have to be thankful for the areas of our lives that are not broken. God always has a plan no matter what the situation looks like. God healed you before you knew anything was broken, before any situation arose in your life. Believe it! Understand it! You are healed. Say it every single day: "In the Name of Jesus, I am healed."

Day 24: Today's Goal

Begin to take better care of your body. Exercise or play outside at least thirty minutes per day. Have fruit today instead of chips when you go to the kitchen to get a snack. Our bodies react to what we put inside them, whether its food or information. Empower your body to stay well by eating healthy. God cares about what we put into our bodies—yes, even when it comes to the foods we eat.

Day 24: From Your Own Perspective

How can you practice better eating habits?

_____
_____
_____
_____

What outdoor activity can you do for thirty minutes per day?

_____
_____
_____
_____

Is there something you are believing God to heal you of?

_____
_____
_____
_____
_____

Day 24: Daily Journal

DAY 25: Creative Power

Today's Confession
Read Aloud

I decree and declare that my creative power through Christ Jesus takes me to places beyond earthly creation. The transformation of my world starts with a change of mind.

Day 25: What It Means to Be and What Is

- Imagination: Creative power.[63]

Day 25: Bread for the Soul

Philippians 4:8 Finally, brethren, whatsoever things are true, whatsoever things are honest, whatsoever things are just, whatsoever things are pure, whatsoever things are lovely, whatsoever things are of good report; if there be any virtue, and if there be any praise, think on these things (KJV).

2 Corinthians 10:3–5 For though we walk in the flesh, we do not war after the flesh: For the weapons of our warfare are not carnal but mighty through God to the pulling down of strong holds; Casting down imaginations, and every high thing that exalteth itself against the knowledge of God, and bringing into captivity every thought to the obedience of Christ (KJV).

Romans 12:2 Do not conform any longer to the pattern of this world, but be transformed by the renewing of your mind.

Then you will be able to test and approve what God's will is—his good, pleasing, and perfect will. (NIV).

Philippians 2:5 Let this mind be in you, which was also in Christ Jesus (KJV).

Day 25: Today's Prayer
Read Aloud

Christ Jesus, I thank You for this day. Lord, I pray that my life will be transformed by Your Spirit. Christ Jesus, uproot every single seed sown into my thought process that is not of You. I pray that the Holy Spirit will plow through the fields of my mind, pulling up the weeds intended to suppress my love and belief in You, Christ Jesus. God of Israel, I call upon Your Name; through Your Son Jesus Christ, tear down every stronghold. I break every negative thought pattern in Jesus' Name. I refute every idea that goes against who God says I am. Lord, make me aware of when the enemy tries to influence my thoughts that I may pray and Your power will destroy the plans of the kingdom of darkness. Christ Jesus, let a divine alarm go off in me when I am listening to or seeing things designed to control and manipulate me. I am Yours, Christ Jesus. God, let this mind be in me that is also in Christ Jesus. Bring my mind to a place where I dwell on things that are honest, just, pure, good, virtuous, and pleasant. Let my mind dwell on ways and reasons to give You praise. I decree and declare that I will have visions and dreams sent from the throne rooms of heaven. Lord, mature and bless the creative power You have placed inside of me. I yield my ideas to God's will in this very moment. Lord, help me to experience the glory of heaven even while I dwell in the earthly realm. In Christ Jesus' Name I pray. Amen

Day 25: Be Encouraged

We all dream of being something great when we grow up—a doctor, lawyer, chef, artist, or dancer; the list goes on and on. Use earthly educational tools, but don't forget to tap into the ones given by heaven. For example, every chef has a signature dish. Every chef wants to create something that has never been tasted before. There are countless recipes in heaven that Christ Jesus would gladly share. This is real. Everything you need is available to you. With your desires come provision. Where did every food ingredient originate from? From the Almighty God.

If you want to be a dancer, there are choreographed moves stored up in heaven that will blow your mind. When you dance, allow the Holy Spirit to take over. If you want to be a doctor, while you are in medical school, ask God to reveal to you hidden things about the human body. No matter how much science knows, God knows tons more. What if God wants to birth a new cure through your mind? If you want to be a musician, ask God to reveal to you new notes and keys. Ask God to share with you the music played in the throne room of heaven. There is a song that *you* are supposed to write. There is a new sound of worship that Christ Jesus wants to birth through you.

There is nothing you want to accomplish in this life that God hasn't prepared you for. God has even prepared you for those genius ideas you don't know are inside you. There is only *one* you in the earth, and God wants to give you something fresh. Your faith carries you to places that may not physically be manifested, yet.

God wants to show the world that if we would just seek Him, the possibilities would be endless. Strive to be who God predestined you to be. God has set things aside for you that no one else has; go after them and take the world by storm. The Bible says in **Ephesians 3:20, "Now unto him who is able to do immeasurably more than we can ask or imagine, according to the power that is at work within us, to him be glory in the church and in Christ Jesus throughout all generations, for ever and ever!(NIV)"**

If you can conceive it in your own mind, God is able to do something with it that cannot be measured, fathomed, and has never been known to man. Think about that, and enter in.

Day 25:
Always and Forever Remember This

- **Man** (being created in the image and likeness of God) has the **Power** (choice/will) to be **Transformed** (believe unto) **Life** or **Death**

- **Renewing** (changing the incoming information) of the **Mind** comes by extending your mind back to its **Eternal State** (through the Word of God/experiencing Christ Jesus).

- **Extension** of the **Mind** is living by the **spirit** in Christ Jesus.

Tools of power are:

- **Tongue** (Proverbs 18:21 The tongue has the power of life and death, and those who love it will eat of its fruit.) (NIV)

- **Mind** (Romans 12:2 ...but be transformed by the renewing of your mind). (NIV)

- **Heart** (Proverbs 23:7 For as he thinketh in his heart, so is he.) (KJV)
(Proverbs 4:23 Above all else, guard your heart, for it is the wellspring of life) (NIV)

Day 25: Today's Goal

Write out what you want to accomplish and the daily goals you are setting to get there.

Day 25: From Your Own Perspective

What have you dreamed of accomplishing that you have never told anyone else? Ask God for understanding of the images you hold in your mind.

_____
_____
_____
_____

Are the visions we see in our mind just images, or are they portals we use to create the world we want to physically see manifested? Wherever your focus goes is where your future will be drawn to. Where is your focus?

_____
_____
_____
_____
_____

Day 25: Daily Journal

DAY 26: Carrier of Glory

Today's Confession
Read Aloud

I decree and declare that my soul is a divine carrier of God's glory. The Lord is a wall of fire around me. Christ Jesus is my glory within. I am the very beat of God's heart. I am the apple of God's eye.

Day 26: Bread for the Soul

Psalms 17:8 Keep me as the apple of your eye; hide me in the shadow of your wings from the wicked who assail me, from my mortal enemies who surround me (NIV).

Zechariah 2:5 "And I myself will be a wall of fire around it," declares the Lord, "and I will be its glory within (NIV)."

Zechariah 2:8 For whoever touches you touches the apple of his eye (NIV).

Day 26: Today's Prayer
Read Aloud

Christ Jesus, I thank You for this day and for all Your blessings. In this moment, Lord, let the heavens and the earth hear my voice. My life is not my own. I no longer live, but Christ lives in me. The life that I live in the body, I live by faith in the Son of God, who loved me and gave Himself up for me **(Galatians 2:20)**. Lord, I am asking You to look inside of me and reconstruct my inner man. My body is the temple of the Holy Spirit; this Spirit is in me because I have received Him from God **(1 Corinthians 6:19)**. Christ Jesus, today I ask You for something that is not only in the storehouses of heaven but in the King of king's personal treasury. Lord, Your secrets are too vast and wide for anyone to fathom, yet I know the mystery of God exists. God, do something in me that has never been done before and will never be seen in the earth again—something that is good, Father, and that brings glory to Your Name. Father, take even the heat from the flame that ever burns in Your temple, and let it rest within my soul. There is a new thing, God; a supernatural thing is taking place right now. I speak into every dimension beyond this world. Let the atmosphere stir itself in preparation to receive the glory of God. Let the elements and every realm between God and man be shaken in this moment that the prayers of my lips may be manifested in the earth. Lord, I raise my hands and say, "Christ Jesus, let Your glory be within." I am now and forever Yours. In Christ Jesus' Name I pray. Amen.

Day 26: Be Encouraged

At times we want to know what life has in store for us next. We want to know when and how certain events are going to take place. Then sometimes we just want life to surprise us. No matter what your plans are, God's final blueprint is ten times better. You may want to be the best brain surgeon in the world; God may give you something that will make you the greatest brain surgeon who ever lived. Look at what God did for Solomon. God gave Solomon wisdom that set him apart from any other king who ever lived **(1 Kings 3:12)**. God uses different means to get each person to his or her destination. Christ Jesus is the common source for everyone who wants to walk not just in greatness but bask in the greatness that exists within the will of God. Christ Jesus has something special planned for your life. God chose you to be alive for this time and season. The fact that the road to your destiny may be different from someone else's doesn't mean a thing. Your process is to prepare you for where you're going. The road may not always be easy, but Christ Jesus is right there through it all. He said He will never leave you or forsake you **(Deuteronomy 31:6)**. Sometimes the heavier the weight, the greater the call on a person's life. Jesus didn't inherit certain glory until the mission was complete. God wants you to come through every trial and test victoriously. Christ Jesus wants you to know that your preparation is not a sign that His plans for you have changed. God gives each person opportunity; it's up to us to take hold of it. Sometimes opportunities do not glisten or look like a gold mine. Those opportunities also come when life's test comes. Those are opportunities to overcome and even move to a new level in God.

With every test, there is a door to graduate to better things. **Isaiah 53:4** says that people considered Jesus stricken by God because of what He was going through, but Jesus was living out His destiny. Jesus Christ carried the ultimate weight, and now He sits at the right hand of the Living God with all power in His hand. **(See. Matthew 28:18)** Decide today that no matter what it looks like to the outside world, you will walk out your purpose and destiny in Christ Jesus.

Day 26: Today's Goal

The bible says in **Proverbs 19:21**, "Many are the plans in a man's heart, but it is the Lord's purpose that prevails." Always run your plans by God. Keep working hard toward your dreams, and allow the Eternal God to unfold the impossibilities of man in your life.

Day 26: From Your Own Perspective

Is there glory in what people may not see as glorious at all?

_____
_____
_____
_____
_____

What if success in God doesn't look like success to people? Would you still walk with God?

_____
_____
_____
_____
_____

Day 26: Daily Journal

DAY 27: Love

Today's Confession
Read Aloud

I decree and declare that I will eternally walk in love. My heart is an ocean where God can pour in, so that I may pour into others. My well will never run dry.

Day 27: Bread for the Soul

1 Corinthians 13:4 Love is patient, love is kind. It does not envy, it does not boast, it is not proud. It is not rude, it is not self-seeking, it is not easily angered, it keeps no records of wrongs. Love does not delight in evil but rejoices with the truth. It always protects, always trusts, always hopes, always perseveres. Love never fails (NIV).

Matthew 5:43–48 You have heard it said, "Love your neighbor and hate your enemy." But I tell you: Love your enemies and pray for those who persecute you, that you may be sons of your father in heaven. He causes his sun to rise on the evil and the good, and sends rain on the righteous and the unrighteous. If you love those who love you, what reward will you get? Are not even tax collectors doing that? And if you greet only your brothers, what are you doing more than others? Do not even pagans do that? Be perfect, therefore, as your heavenly Father is perfect (NIV).

1 Corinthians 13:13 And now these three remain: faith, hope, and love. But the greatest of these is love (NIV).

Matthew 22:36–40 "Teacher, which is the greatest commandment in the Law?" Jesus replied: "Love the Lord your God with all your heart and with all your soul and with all your mind. This is the greatest commandment. And the second is like it: Love your neighbor as yourself. All the Law and the Prophets hang on these two commandments" (NIV).

1 John 4:7–12 Dear friends, let us love one another, for love comes from God. Everyone who loves has been born of God and knows God. Whoever does not love does not know God, because God is love. This is how God showed his love among us: He sent his one and only Son into the world that we might live through him. This is love: not that we loved God, but that he first loved us and sent his Son as an atoning sacrifice for our sins. Dear friends, since God so loved us, we also ought to love one another. No one has ever seen God; but if we love one another, God lives in us and his love is made complete in us (NIV).

1 John 4:16 God is Love. Whoever lives in love lives in God and God in him (NIV).

Day 27: Today's Prayer
Read Aloud

Christ Jesus, I give You praise this day for Your loving kindness. Lord, please fill my heart with divine love that I may love others as You have commanded. Teach me the meaning of loving my enemies. God I know that You are love. I pray that as You fill me with Your spirit, and love will take its rightful place in my heart. I pray that I will learn the rhythms of Your heart, Christ Jesus. I thank You for the ability to share love with those around me. God, as You breathed the breath of life into man, breath the aroma of Your love in me. In Jesus' Name I pray. Amen.

Day 27: Be Encouraged

Love is a lifestyle. Sometimes walking in love comes easy, and sometimes it doesn't. The Holy Spirit teaches us how to walk in love and also how to love ourselves. True love stretches us. True love for someone or something exists without reason. That describes the way God loves each one of us. God's love for humanity can't be explained. Why? Because love in the human mind usually has limits, yet God put no limitations on His love, ever. The Bible says that nothing in all creation is able to separate us from the love of God **(See. Romans 8:38–39)**. Love stretches us into the eternal.

You need the assistance of Christ Jesus to keep on loving when you simply don't want to. We have talked about forgiveness, which has everything to do with love. The next time you are looking for a way to get over what someone did to you, ask Christ Jesus, "In this situation, what do I do to walk in love?" God wants to greatly increase your capacity to love.

Sometimes that happens by allowing you to be in a situation in which you have the choice to either resent a person or love them anyway. Be thankful for the people who seem to push your buttons because you can mature in those situations—even if that means loving them and walking away to avoid confrontation. Life will teach you about love in one way or another. Life can teach us humans how much we need love, how powerful it is, that it is a serum for healing, and what happens when humans don't walk in love or choose to live without it. Renounce hate, and make love the air that your actions breathe.

Day 27: Today's Goal

Be nice to someone today who usually gives you a hard time. You can just say hello or compliment them on the shirt they are wearing.

Day 27: From Your Own Perspective

What does true love mean to you?

_____
_____
_____
_____
_____

Does your definition of love resemble God's definition of love?

_____
_____
_____
_____
_____

Is love by God's standards a responsibility, a command from God, or both? As a child of God, do any of us have a choice regarding whether we love others?

_____
_____
_____
_____

Day 27: Daily Journal

DAY 28: Seeds

Today's Confession
Read Aloud

I decree and declare that I am generous, thoughtful, and one who sows into others.

Day 28: What It Means to Be and What Is

- Generous: Liberal in giving or sharing.[64]

- Thoughtful: Having or showing regard for others; considerate.[65]

Day 28: Bread for the Soul

Acts 20:35 Remembering the words the Lord Jesus himself said: It is more blessed to give than to receive (NIV).

Psalm 112:5 Good will come to him who is generous and lends freely, who conducts his affairs with justice (NIV).

Matthew 25:31–46 When the Son of man comes in his glory, and all angels with him, he will sit on his throne in heavenly glory. All the nations will be gathered before him, and he will separate the people one from another as a shepherd separates the sheep from the goats. He will put the sheep on his right and the goats on his left. Then the King will say to those on his right, "Come you who are blessed by my Father; take your inheritance, the kingdom prepared for you since the creation of the world. For I was hungry and you gave me something to eat, I was thirsty and you gave me something to drink, I was a stranger and you invited me in, I needed clothes and you clothed me, I was sick and you looked after me, I was in prison and you came to visit me." Then the righteous will answer him, "Lord, when did we see you hungry and feed you, or thirsty and give you something to drink? When did we see you a stranger and invite you in, or needing clothes and clothe you? When did we see you sick or in prison and go to visit you?" The King will reply, "I tell you the truth, whatever you did for one of the least of these brothers of mine, you did for me." Then he will say to those on his left, "Depart from me, you who are cursed, into the eternal fire prepared for the devil and his angels. For I was hungry and you gave me nothing to eat, I was thirsty and you gave me nothing to drink, I was a stranger and you did not invite me in. I needed clothes and you did not clothe me, I was sick and in prison and you did not look after me." They will also answer, "Lord, when did we see you hungry or thirsty or a stranger or needing clothes or sick or in prison, and did not help you?" He will reply, "I tell you the truth, whatever you did not do for one of the least of these, you did not do for me." Then they will go away to eternal punishment, but the righteous to eternal life.

Day 28: Today's Prayer
Read Aloud

Christ Jesus, thank You for grace. I pray, Lord, that You will continue to supply my every need according to Your riches and glory. **(Philippians 4:19)** Lord, I pray that You will bless my spirit with the gift of hospitality. Lord, I pray that I will always give based on Your will for that time. I will give when prompted by the Holy Spirit. Lord, when You command me to lend a hand to my neighbor, I decree and declare that I will act quickly. I will give with the right motives. I decree and declare that the hand of God will guide me. Lord, I submit even the materialistic things I have to ministry. Christ, I pray that my life and belongings will be a blessing to others. Lord, grant me the opportunity to be a blessing to someone else. In Christ Jesus' Name I pray. Amen.

Day 28: Be Encouraged

God's blessings are endless. It's a blessing to have life in our bodies. It's a blessing when we have food to eat. It's even a blessing to be able to speak. No matter what blessings we have, God always expects us to give thanks. God also expects us to be a blessing to others. So if it is a blessing to speak, God expects us to use our mouths to uplift those around us and to pronounce blessings over their lives. If we are at school sitting next to the kid who doesn't have supplies, it's OK to share a pencil or a few sheets of paper just to be kind. As we bless others, Christ Jesus continually blesses us.

As blessings are distributed from heaven to us, they are to be distributed from us to others. Let say, for example, that God blesses you with a new car when you get older. Be a blessing to others with that car, maybe by giving them a ride to the grocery store or church. Show God that you are more than willing to give back whatever

He gives you. Allow the Holy Spirit to lead you in how to be a blessing.

Again, look at the woman who washed Jesus' feet. She was poor, and that jar of perfume was all she had (**Luke** 7:37–50). She used the last of what she had to bring glory to Jesus Christ. What really mattered wasn't so much what the woman had but what she did with what she had. We never know how glorious one act of giving can be. What we may see as insignificant may mean the world to somebody else. It does the heart good to put a smile on somebody else's face. That why the Bible says it's more blessed to give than to receive. (**Acts** 20:35) Giving does something wonderful for an individual on the inside. Try it out today! (Ask parents' permission and advice when being a blessing to others.)

Day 28: Today's Goal

Be an unexpected blessing to somebody else today. If you're home, go help your younger siblings with their chores. If you see someone at school struggling to carry a book, help out a little. Sometimes the best thing we can give are not material things but our time.

Day 28: From Your Own Perspective

What has God given you that you could use to be a blessing to someone else?

_____
_____
_____
_____
_____

Is it better to expect something in return for what we do for others or seek to glorify the Name of Jesus Christ?

_____
_____
_____
_____
_____

Day 28: Daily Journal

DAY 29: Salvation

Today's Confession
Read Aloud

I decree and declare that I am saved and have received salvation through Jesus Christ's blood. I am a citizen of the Kingdom of God. I am forgiven.

Day 29: Bread for the Soul

Romans 10:9–13 That if you confess with your mouth, "Jesus is Lord," and believe in your heart that God raised him from the dead, you will be saved. For it is with your heart that you believe and are justified, and it is with your mouth that you confess and are saved. As the scripture says, "Anyone who trust in him will never be put to shame." For there is no difference between Jew and Gentile—the same Lord is Lord of all and richly blesses those who call on him, for "Everyone who calls on the name of the Lord will be saved."

Hebrews 4:15–16 Therefore, since we have a great high priest who has gone through the heavens, Jesus the Son of God, let us hold firmly to the faith we profess. For we do not have a high priest who is unable to sympathize with our weaknesses, but we have one who has been tempted in every way, just as we are—yet was without sin. Let us then approach the throne of grace with confidence, so that we may receive mercy and find grace to help us in our time of need.

John 6:35 and 37 Then Jesus declared…"All that the Father gives me will come to me, and whoever comes to me I will never drive away."

Romans 8:11 And if the Spirit of him who raised Jesus from the dead is living in you, he who raised Christ from the dead will also give life to your mortal bodies through his Spirit, who lives in you (NIV).

Day 29: Today's Prayer
Read Aloud

Christ Jesus, thank You for dying on the cross for me. Lord, I am a sinner. Christ Jesus, please come into my heart and be the Lord and Savior of my life. Please forgive me of all my sins against You, even the ones that are unknown. Wash away the guilt, Lord, and the condemnation. I know that, as it says in **Romans 8:1, Therefore, there is now no condemnation for those who are in Christ Jesus.** I confess with my mouth that Jesus is Lord, Master, Ruler, and Savior of the world. I believe in my heart that God raised Jesus from the dead on the third day. I know that the same power that raised Jesus from the dead is now living in me. **(Romans 8:11)** Lord, I know that You are not concerned with the mistakes of my past; You desire to bring me to a bright future. I accept Your Salvation, Christ Jesus; I am now and forever Yours. I thank You that I am saved by Your grace. In this moment, I place my heart in Your hands. I am saved. In Christ Jesus' Name I pray. Amen.

Day 29: Be Encouraged

Guess what? If you just prayed that prayer, you are now saved, and have received the gift of salvation. You just welcomed Jesus into your life and heart. It's what heaven has longed for. God is in your corner and will do whatever is necessary to see that you make it. God already did that when He sent His only Son to die on the cross for our sins. Salvation is a gift from God that is *free to all.* Being saved is being welcomed into a new family that is too big to number. It's receiving the gift of eternal life, through Chris Jesus. God sees you as His child, and He knows you by name. Christ Jesus is the *only* way to God. Jesus said in **John 14:6, "I am the way and the truth and the life. No one comes to the Father except through me. If you really knew me, you would know my Father as well. From now on, you do know him and have seen him (NIV)."**

No matter where you have been or what you have done, His grace is sufficient. **(2 Corinthians 12:9)** God doesn't dwell on your past so you don't do it either. You are forgiven. Christ Jesus is waiting for you, He has been asking about you. Heaven has a message for you, and it is this: Welcome home!

Day 29: Today's Goal

Forget your past! Today is a new day. By praying the prayer mentioned above, you have given your life to Christ Jesus. Everything is going to be alright. You are free. Simply tell Christ Jesus, thank you.

Day 29: From Your Perspective

What are you looking forward to most being a child of the Most High God?

_____
_____
_____
_____

Day 29: Daily Journal

DAY 30: Holy Spirit

Today's Confession
Read Aloud

I decree and declare that the Holy Spirit guides me and lives inside of me. My ears are open to hear what He is saying. Rivers of living water will flow from within me.

Day 30: Bread for the Soul

John 7:37-38 ...Jesus stood and said in a loud voice, "If anyone is thirsty, let him come to me and drink. Whoever believes in me, as the Scripture has said, streams of living water will flow from within him."

John 14:15–16 If you love me, you will obey what I command. And I will ask the Father, and he will give you another Counselor to be with you forever, the Spirit of truth. The world cannot accept him, because it neither sees him or knows him. But you know him, for he lives with you and will be in you (NIV).

John 16:7 But I tell you the truth: It is for your good that I am going away. Unless I go away, the Counselor will not come to you; but if I go, I will send him to you (NIV).

Ephesians 1:13–14 And you also were included in Christ when you heard the Word of truth, the gospel of your salvation. Having believed, you were marked in him with a seal, the promised Holy Spirit, who is a deposit guaranteeing our inheritance until the redemption of those who are God's possession—to the praise of his glory (NIV).

Psalm 37:23–27 The steps of a good man are ordered by the Lord: and he delighteth in his way. Though he fall, he shall not be utterly cast down: for the Lord upholdeth him with his hand. I have been young, and now am old; yet I have not seen the righteous forsaken, nor his seed begging bread. He is ever merciful, and lendeth; and his seed is blessed. Depart from evil and do good; and dwell evermore (KJV).

Acts 2:38 Peter replied, "Repent and be baptized, every one of you, in the name of Jesus Christ for the forgiveness of your sins. And you will receive the gift of the Holy Spirit" (NIV).

Day 30: Today's Prayer
Read Aloud

Christ Jesus, I thank You for the gift You left here with humanity. Jesus, please fill me until I overflow. Holy Spirit, please come into my heart. Holy Spirit, I pray that You will always speak to me and that my spirit will be attentive to Your promptings. Fill me with wisdom and guide my steps. Reveal to me where I am to be established in this season. Holy Spirit, I request that You intercede for me. Holy Spirit, be my Counselor and friend. Holy Spirit, give me a new spiritual tongue; teach me to engage in spiritual warfare through prayer and supplication. Christ Jesus, please set Your seal on me with the promised Holy Spirit. Let it remain until the day of redemption. In Christ Jesus' Name I pray. Amen.

Day 30: Be Encouraged

Christ Jesus left the Holy Spirit here with us as a Counselor. The Holy Spirit should be your best friend. He is that little voice inside that tells you to make the right decision. The Holy Spirit is very kind and mild. He shows up when we least expect it and was given to us as a guide, guiding us on a road that leads to God's perfect will for our lives. Let the Holy Spirit come and construct every aspect of your life. Sometimes we have to be quiet to hear what He is saying. Remember, sometimes in life it's not that God isn't speaking but rather that we aren't listening.

Day 30: Today's Goal

Talk to the Holy Spirit daily. He is waiting for you to ask for whatever you need. The Holy Spirit is here to give us understanding and to push us on when we want throw in the towel.

Day 30: From Your Own Perspective

The Father, Son, and Holy Spirit are one—better known as the Trinity. What time have you set aside just for the four of you to fellowship?

_____

_____

Day 30: Daily Journal

DAY 31: Freedom

Today's Confession
Read Aloud

I decree and declare that I am free. I am free from every stronghold of the enemy. I am free from everything that opposes the divine nature God has placed within me.

Day 31: Bread for the Soul

John 8:36 So if the Son sets you free, you will be free indeed (NIV).

Galatians 3:13–14 Christ redeemed us from the curse of the law by becoming a curse for us, for it is written: "Cursed is everyone who is hung from a tree." He redeemed us in order that the blessing of Abraham might come to the Gentiles through Christ Jesus, so that by faith we might receive the promise of the Spirit (NIV).

Psalms 118:5 In my anguish I cried to the Lord, and he answered by setting me free (NIV).

Psalms 119:5 I will walk about in freedom, for I have sought out your precepts (NIV).

Romans 6:22-23 But now that you have been set free from sin and have become slaves to God, the benefit you reap leads to holiness, and the result is eternal life. For the wages of sin is death, but the gift of God is eternal life in Christ Jesus our Lord (NIV).

Day 31: Today's Prayer
Read Aloud

Lord, I thank You for standing in the gap for me. Christ Jesus, You have redeemed me from the curse of the law. Through this act on my behalf, I receive the blessings of Abraham. Lord, Your Word says the just live by faith. **(Habakkuk 2:4)** Help me to believe, Father, in what I can't physically see. I am free from all pain and from every chain of the kingdom of darkness. Lord, I call forth the life You have intended for me to live. I call it forth from the throne rooms of heaven. Lord, I know that no matter where this life takes me, You are with me. I decree and declare that the past is over. I know that once You have settled a thing, it is finished. In Christ Jesus' Name I pray. Amen.

Day 31: Be Encouraged

The kingdom of God is a place where freedom reigns in Christ Jesus. God wants His perfect will to exist on earth as it does in heaven. God wants you to be free of every struggle and every chain of the past or present. Christ Jesus wants you to be completely free. Freedom comes with a choice to change and a choice to let go. I want you to know there is absolutely *nothing* God won't free you from. You never have to be ashamed no matter what you are dealing with on the inside. God *wants* you to come to Him. He prefers that you cast all your cares on Him.

(1 Peter 5:7, Psalm 55:22) He sees all and knows exactly where you are. Jesus still holds out His hands out to you welcoming you in. Try Him.

1 Peter 5:7 says, "Humble yourself therefore under the mighty hand of God, that he may exalt you in due time: Casting all your care upon him: for he careth for you" (KJV).

No matter where you are in your life, you don't have to carry that burden alone. Let Christ Jesus help you. Start confessing every day, "Through Christ Jesus, I am free." Make daily choices that support the confession you are making over yourself. Say whatever it is you want to be free from. As you speak it, you call it into existence. Then you will begin to believe it, and as you believe it, you begin to live it out. Your freedom is always one choice away.

Day 31: Today's Goal

If you have a struggle in your life, take power over it. For the next thirty days, say, "I decree and declare that Christ Jesus has freed me from (*whatever you struggle is*)." Remember that your words have power; use that tool to your advantage.

Day 31: From Your Own Perspective

What is God trying to free you from in this season?

_____
_____
_____
_____

Is it better to have peace in God walking in freedom, or have comfort in the flesh while still doing the wrong things? Discomfort in the flesh is sometimes manifest peace within ones soul.

_____
_____
_____
_____

Is there a root or cause to your struggle? The Holy Spirit will help you deal with the struggle and also the reason it is there. Sometimes you may not know what the root is, but that doesn't prevent the Holy Spirit from doing a work in your life.

_____
_____

Day 31: Daily Journal

DAY 32: Safe In His Arms

Today's Confession
Read Aloud

I decree and declare that I am spiritually, mentally, and physically safe through the blood of Christ Jesus. No weapon formed against me shall prosper.

Day 32: Bread for the Soul

Isaiah 54:17 No weapon that is formed against thee shall prosper; and every tongue that shall rise up against thee in judgment thou shalt condemn. This is the heritage of the servants of the Lord, and their righteousness is of me, saith the Lord (KJV).

Psalms 23 The Lord is my shepherd; I shall not want. He maketh me to lie down in green pastures: he leadeth me beside the still waters. He restoreth my soul: he leadeth me in the paths of righteousness for his name's sake. Yea, though I walk through the valley of the shadow of death, I will fear no evil: for thou art with me; thy rod and thy staff, they comfort me. Thou preparest a table before me in the presence of mine enemies: thou anointest my head with oil; my cup runneth over. Surely goodness and mercy shall follow me all the days of my life: and I will dwell in the house of the Lord forever (KJV).

Psalms 91 He that dwelleth in the secret place of the most High shall abide under the shadow of the Almighty. I will say of the Lord, He is my refuge and my fortress: my God; in him will I trust. Surely he shall deliver thee from the snare of the fowler, and from the noisome pestilence. He shall cover thee with his feathers, and under his wings shalt thou trust: his truth shall be thy shield and buckler. Thou shalt not be afraid for the terror by night; nor for the arrow that flieth by day; Nor for the pestilence that walketh in darkness; nor for the destruction that wasteth at noonday. A thousand may fall at thy side and ten thousand at thy right hand; but it shall not come nigh thee. Only with thine eyes shalt thou behold and see the reward of the wicked. Because thou hast made the Lord, which is my refuge, even the most High, thy habitation. There shall no evil befall thee, neither shall any plague come nigh thy dwelling. For he shall give his angels charge over thee, to keep thee in all thy ways. They shall bear thee up in their hands, lest thou dash thy foot against a stone. Thou shalt tread upon the lion and adder, the young lion and the dragon shalt thou trample under feet. Because he hath set his love upon me, therefore will I deliver him: I will set him on high, because he hath known my name. He shall call upon me, and I will answer him: I will be with him in trouble; I will deliver him, and honor him. With long life I will satisfy him, and shew him my salvation (KJV).

Day 32: Today's Prayer
Read Aloud

Lord, I thank You for ever watching over me. I thank You for heaven's surveillance over my life and being. Christ Jesus, protect me from danger seen and unseen. I plead Psalms 91, Psalms 23, and the blood of Jesus over myself this day. Lord, go before me as a cloud by day and as a flame of fire by night. **(Exodus 13:21)** Jesus, I pray that, as it says in **Psalms 46:5**, You will be within me so I will not fall. God, please help me at the break of day. Lord, I thank You also for the battles You fight for me daily in the spirit realm. I decree and declare that the Holy Spirit surrounds me as a consuming fire. I bind every plan of the kingdom of darkness through the blood of Jesus. The plans of the kingdom of darkness will not succeed in my life. Lord, I speak into the spirit realm, and I pray that God's wind of judgment will disrupt the arsenal of the kingdom of darkness. Every tool the enemy planned to use is destroyed though the blood of Jesus Christ. I call upon the Holy Spirit to disrupt every surveillance the enemy tried to keep over me or my family. Jesus, protect me from individuals who attack others with their words. In the name of Jesus, I bind the spirit of bullying not just in my school but in this nation. You have commanded all humanity to walk in love and to be a light to the world. Lord, I am Yours. God, cover me with Your right hand and hide under the shadow of your wings. (Psalms 17:8) In Christ Jesus' Name I pray. Amen.

Day 32: Be Encouraged

Every day when you wake up, ask God to give His angels charge over you. Christ Jesus will protect you, and He is always looking after you. When you go to school, pray and thank Christ Jesus for covering you in His blood. Plead **Psalms 91** and **Psalms 23** over yourself every day. Make good choices to keep yourself from harm. As you depend on God, also do the right things. We have God's grace, but we must also use wisdom. Even Jesus, when being tempted by the devil, did not do anything to put God to the test **(Luke 4:9–12)**. Never put yourself in harm's way just to see of God will act. I want you to know again that God desires for you to be safe at all times. If you don't remember anything else, just keep repeating that *no weapon formed against you shall prosper.* If you are dealing with a bully at school, tell God about it. Also, inform your parents and those in authority over you. Talk to someone, you are not alone. If you feel that someone is giving you a hard time and you are not sure how to handle it, welcome God into the situation—all you have to do is ask. You are the apple of God's eye, and Christ Jesus is forever watching over you. The bible says in **2 Chronicles 16:9**, **"For the eyes of the Lord range throughout the earth to strengthen those whose** hearts are fully committed to him (NIV)." You are never alone.

Day 32: Today's Goal

Write out a list of five things you can do to keep yourself safe. Today make a choice not to put yourself or others at risk in any way—even with your words.

Day 32: From Your Own Perspective

Do you ever hear God's voice trying to change your course of direction? Even in the little things—for example, the Holy Spirit may say, "Don't go to this particular party" or "Don't hang out at this particular friend's house today." We have to listen for God's voice because sometimes He may instruct us not to do a particular thing we have done one hundred times before. Sometimes you may feel that you're missing out. But is it better to listen to God's voice or enjoy a temporary pleasure that can have negative results?

_____
_____
_____

What can you do to keep others safe around you? Safety is not just physically being OK. We as humans need safety for our heart, mind, emotions, and spirit. What can you do today to promote safety in someone else's life?

_____
_____
_____
_____
_____

Day 32: Daily Journal

DAY 33: Trust God

Today's Confession
Read Aloud

I decree and declare that I trust God with my very life and all that I am. I will never withhold any part of myself from Christ Jesus.

Day 33: Bread for the Soul

Proverbs 3:5 Trust in the Lord with all your heart and lean not to your own understanding; in all your ways acknowledge him, and he will make your paths straight. Do not be wise in your own eyes: fear the Lord and shun evil. This will bring health to your body and nourishment to your bones (NIV).

Isaiah 40:28-31 Do you not know? Have you not heard? The Lord is the everlasting God, the Creator of the ends of the earth. He will not grow tired or weary, and his understanding no one can fathom. He gives strength to the weary and increases the power of the weak. Even youths grow tired and weary and young men stumble and fall; but those who hope in the Lord will renew their strength. They will soar on wings like eagles; they will run and not grow weary, they will walk and not be faint (NIV).

2 Chronicles 20:15 ...This is what the Lord says to you: 'Do not be afraid or discouraged because of this vast army. For the battle is not yours, but God's (NIV)'

Day 33: Today's Prayer
Read Aloud

Christ Jesus, great is Your faithfulness in all the earth. **(Lamentations 3:23)** Lord, no matter what the circumstance, I will trust You. Christ Jesus, I trust You with my life, spirit, and entire existence. Lord, You see all things; please help my faith and grant me the grace to believe. Your Word says the righteous live by faith. **(Romans 1:17)** So, Lord, this day I command my spirit and mind to put faith in Your Word. Jesus please take away all my doubt, and replace it with unwavering faith. I command my beliefs to come into divine alignment with Your will, Christ Jesus. I know You have not given us the spirit of fear but of love, power, and a sound mind **(2 Timothy 1:7)**. So as I trust You, Lord, my soul will be at peace. In Jesus' Name I pray. Amen.

Day 33: Be Encouraged

Give God everything that you have. No matter how precious something or even someone is to you, entrust them to the Lord Christ Jesus. Christ Jesus can do more with the little or much than we could in a billion lifetimes. God longs for His children to trust Him through thick and thin. Christ Jesus wants you to know that if He made you a promise, it will come to pass. In the Bible, God promised Abraham a son **(Genesis 15:1–5, Genesis 18:10)**.

Abraham's wife had been barren into old age, so it meant the world to Abraham when his son Isaac finally came. Then after Isaac was born some time later God told Abraham to sacrifice him (Genesis 22:1–19). You will see that God spared Isaac in that story. God needed to know that Abraham would trust Him, even if it seemed that he was going to lose what God had promised him. God wants the same from each one us. No matter how much pain may seem to be ahead or how hard a certain season may be, will we trust that He has a plan? Sometimes God will allow us to get right on the edge, and then He pulls us back. God wants to know there are no limits to our faith or our love for Him.

Day 33: Today's Goal

Maybe you have been fighting a particular battle in your life for quite some time. It may be that you are trying to get someone to see something a certain way or even trying to bring great change into your own life. Give that situation over to Christ Jesus today. When we turn our battles over to God, we are putting our carnal weapons down and allowing Him to step in and take control. Christ Jesus can do more with people and situations than you can. So lay your burden on the altar today, walk away, and leave it there. Don't pick it back up through actions or even by what you say. Before you complain or ponder how bad it seems stop, worship God and give Him glory because the victory is already won. In addition, the worship of Christ Jesus is the morphine to life's pain.

Day 33: From Your Own Perspective

What do you need to do in your personal life to stop fighting the battles God should be fighting?

___
___
___
___

Is there a friend or anyone in your family who is fighting a battle and you need God to step in?

___
___
___
___

What confession have you been making over your situation? Have you been confessing that it will get better or worse? One way to indirectly say a situation will get worse is to complain. In **Philippians 2:14**, the bible says, **"Do everything without complaining or arguing, so that you may become blameless and pure, children of God without fault in a crooked and depraved generation, in which you shine like stars of the universe (NIV)."**

Christ Jesus doesn't desire for us to give more glory to the situation than we do to Him. Let your mouth give God glory; don't glorify the situation by complaining.

_____
_____
_____
_____
_____

Day 33: Daily Journal

DAY 34: Living Flame

Today's Confession
Read Aloud

I decree and declare that I am a world changer. I am a general in the Kingdom of God. I know that heaven will remember my name. My life will be a divine testimony that eternity will never forget.

Day 34: Bread for the Soul

Matthew 5:14–16 You are the light of the world. A city on a hill cannot be hidden. Neither do people light a lamp and put it under a bowl. Instead they put it on its stand, and it gives light to everyone in the house. In the same way, let your light shine before men that they may see your good deeds and praise your Father in heaven (NIV).

Matthew 24:13–14 But he who stands firm to the end will be saved. And this gospel of the kingdom will be preached in all the world as a testimony to all nations, and then the end will come (NIV).

Mark 16:15 He said to them, "Go into all the world and preach the good news to all creation." (NIV).

Day 34: Today's Prayer
Read Aloud

Christ Jesus, I thank You for Your power and love. Lord, I pray that You will use my life to affect not just those around me but regions and territories. Lord, show me how to share the gospel of Jesus Christ with the entire world; let my life be my ministry. In all that I say, do, and even think, I pray that people will see Your light in me, Christ Jesus. Lord, I pray that You will begin to use me wherever my feet may tread. Greatness in You is bringing glory to Your Name. Yahweh, I will forever give You praise for choosing me and letting me be born for such a time as this. I can do all things through You, Christ Jesus **(Philippians 4:13)**. Lord, I know that Your love has taken the world by storm throughout the ages. I yield myself to You; may Your love shine through me. In Christ Jesus' Name I pray. Amen.

Day 34: Be Encouraged

Your being here on earth was ordained before time began. Shout from the rooftops that Christ Jesus is Lord. Be God's mouthpiece and instrument. God is preparing you. God had to prepare Moses to bring Israel out of captivity, just as He had to prepare David to become king of Israel. God had to prepare Joseph to be not just a leader but also a humble leader. All these people went through a process, or what some may perceive as trouble, before they stepped into what God had for them. They had to endure what others did not. But that did not mean God wasn't with them. The bible says in **Matthew 7:13–14, "Enter through the narrow gate. For wide is the gate and broad is the road that leads to destruction, and many enter through it. But small is the gate and narrow the road that leads to life, and only a few find it."**

As a world changer, you may go through what others do not. God wants you to take the road less traveled. In the Bible, Jesus says, **"In this world you will have trouble. But take heart! I have overcome the world." John 16:33.** If there is one thing God is reminding humanity to do through this generation, it is to stand and endure no matter what the cost. You're going to change the world, and it starts right where you are. One decision, one process, one victory at a time. Christ Jesus didn't change the world just by coming to earth and doing miracles; He changed the world through His death. Changing the world doesn't always come wrapped in a package that glorifies us; rather, it relates to what we are willing to sacrifice for the sake of the Cross. Christ Jesus taught us a lesson in what He did. The greatest inheritance came through what He suffered. Christ Jesus is with you, and He will be until the very end. You will be triumphant. You will be victorious.

Day 34: Today's Goal

Strive to come to a place in your relationship with God that no matter what He asks of you, you will go. When we are down to nothing, that's when God expects us to give Him everything. Those who withhold none of themselves from Christ Jesus are in a place to receive everything He promised.

Day 34: From Your Own Perspective

What can you give God today that you have never given Him before?

_____
_____
_____
_____
_____

Will you enlist in God's army as someone who will march with Him and fight for His will?

_____
_____
_____
_____
_____

Day 34: Daily Journal

DAY 35: Zeal

Today's Confession
Read Aloud

I decree and declare that I have great zeal for the Lord. My soul is on fire for the Eternal God. I am one who worships God in spirit and in truth.

Day 35: Bread for the Soul

Romans 12:11-12 Never be lacking in zeal, but keep your spiritual fervor, serving the Lord. Be joyful in hope, patient in affliction, faithful in prayer (NIV).

Hebrews 12:28-29 Therefore, since we are receiving a kingdom that cannot be shaken, let us be thankful, and so worship God acceptably with reverence and awe, for our God is a consuming fire (NIV).

1 Thessalonians 5:16-24 Be joyful always; pray continually; give thanks in all circumstances, for this is God's will for you in Christ Jesus. Do not put out the Spirit's fire; do not treat prophecies with contempt. Test everything. Hold on to good. Avoid every kind of evil. May God himself, the God of peace, sanctify you through and through. May your whole spirit, soul, and body be kept blameless at the coming of our Lord Jesus Christ. The one who calls you is faithful, and he will do it (NIV).

John 4:23-24 Yet a time is coming and has now come when the true worshippers will worship the Father in spirit and in truth, for they are the kind of worshippers the Father seeks.

God is a spirit, and his worshippers must worship in spirit and in truth (NIV).

Day 35: Today's Prayer
Read Aloud

Christ Jesus, I thank You for this day. I give you glory, Lord, for your goodness to me. Lord, I pray you will give me a new zeal for you. Holy Spirit, kindle something in my heart for the Lord Jesus Christ that cannot be quenched. I call forth the four winds of heaven right now to fan the flame in my life. I speak into the atmosphere beyond this world and pray that every trap of the kingdom of darkness will be torched. Lord please send forth your angels who serve You in holiness to do warfare on my behalf. Christ Jesus send the chariots of fire to bring back everything the enemy has stolen. I decree and declare that every barricade the enemy has tried to set up in my life is trampled upon by the Spirit of the Living God. Lord, you are my reason for living. You are my biggest fan, my champion, and my friend. God, You are a consuming fire; please burn in me. In Christ Jesus' Name I pray. Amen.

Day 35: Be Encouraged

Whatever we decide to do in this life, we always have some type of motivation. Some things seem to come naturally to us; we do them because we simply want to. That is where God wants each one of us to be when we are serving Him. God wants the desire to become natural to us, because technically it is. No matter how a person may feel right now, God can kindle that desire in him or her for more of Him and to experience His glory. The truth is that everyone in this world is looking for God. That's why there are billions of people searching for the next best thing to make them feel whole. Some people put that dependency on a job or even a car. We all have a space in us that is designed for Christ Jesus alone. A place that only God can fill. When a person who has everything still feels empty, it is because the place where Christ Jesus is supposed to dwell is crying out in them. Continue to ask God to ignite the fire in you, and may the grace in that flame carry you until the very end.

Day 35: Today's Goal

What do you love most about God? What sparks your interest in Him? Where there is intrigue, a desire springs forth to know more. Build on your desire for God.

Day 35: From Your Own Perspective

What is it that you want heaven to take notice of in your life?

_____
_____
_____
_____
_____

Day 35: Daily Journal

DAY 36: Family and Unity

Today's Confession
Read Aloud

I decree and declare that Christ Jesus is the Lord and Head of my family. I am loyal and thankful for those God has given me as family. My family is growing in unity every day.

Day 36: Bread for the Soul

Jeremiah 31:1 At the same time, saith the Lord, will I be the God of all the families of Israel, and they shall be my people (KJV).

Psalm 107:41 But he lifted the needy out of their affliction and increased their families' life flocks (NIV).

Psalm 68:6 God sets the lonely in families... (NIV).

Joshua 24:15 But as for me and my household, we will serve the Lord (NIV).

Day 36: Today's Prayer
Read Aloud

Christ Jesus, I thank You for the family You have given me in Your kingdom, and I also give thanks for my earthly family. Lord, You know better than anyone the needs of my family. Christ Jesus, please lift my family out of every affliction. Lord, I pray that, as it says in **1 Chronicles 4:10**, You will bless my family and enlarge our territory; let Your hand be with us and keep us from harm so that we will be free from pain (NIV). Christ Jesus, You see each person's heart. Lord, I thank You for unifying my family. Christ Jesus, help us to have the grace to love each other. Lord, I just pray that my sins and those of my family be forgiven, cast into the sea of forgetfulness. God of Israel, be the God of my family, and we will be Your people. Christ Jesus, usher my family into a new season. Reveal Yourself to us in a whole new way. Christ Jesus, I pray that You will bless the leadership of my home. Let Your Spirit continually speak to us. Christ Jesus, I pray that Your Spirit and the Holy Spirit will rest in my home. Let Your glory dwell here. Right now, Father, I place a hedge of protection around each member of my household. I pray that no weapon formed against my family will prosper. God of Israel, surround this house and every member in it with Your fire and love. Lord, please post Your holy angels around this household so they will keep watch. Christ Jesus, let Your blood be on the post of every door in this home, including the front door. In Christ Jesus' Name I pray. Amen.

Day 36: Be Encouraged

God loves your family. God knows that no family is perfect, but His grace is sufficient. As a young person in your home, you can stand up and take leadership. For instance, if people rarely say, "I love you" in your house, start telling your mom and dad that you love them every morning before you go to school. If you have a younger sibling who needs help in a particular area, step up and help. God takes note of how siblings treat one another. He expects all of us to conduct ourselves in a way that is pleasing to Him.

Sometimes we see the lack in certain areas, and it is there that God expects us to become the increase. In other words, God wants you to be the difference. Remain obedient and respectful to your parents at all times. Cherish the relationship you have with your siblings. If you don't have the best communication with a brother or sister, make an effort to repair the relationship. When Jesus said to love your neighbor as yourself **(Matthew 22:39)**, that includes your brothers and sisters; there are no exceptions.

There are times your family will have to band together. Sometimes family will be all you have, so give God thanks for your family today. Even though there may be issues, ask the Spirit of the Living God to sweep through your home and correct the wrongs. You be the one to give heaven permission to intervene in your home. You be the one who continually reminds God how much your family needs Him. The next time an issue arises, pray right then for Christ Jesus to step in. Simply ask the Holy Spirit, "Please come now." It's not your job to change people, you are to be an example of Christ Jesus by how you live.

God knows that families are blended; sometimes our guardians aren't the ones who birthed us, but God has still given us family. Some families include grandparents and grandchildren. Others families consist of aunts, uncles, nieces, cousins, and nephews. Some families are made up of brothers and sisters. Regardless of your family dynamic, love your family and continually thank God for them.

You are a star, so shine, even in your home. As you shine in Christ, may you be an example to others around you. And remember, along with your earthly family, you have a heavenly one. The Eternal God is looking out for you.

Day 36: Today's Goal

Tell each family member today that you love them, and give them one nice compliment. Say a prayer for your family every single day. Make it a point to do one nice thing for one family member every day. Even if it's just helping your little brother learn to tie his shoes. The little things go a long way.

Day 36: From Your Own Perspective

What activity would you like your family to do more of together?

_____
_____
_____
_____
_____

What do you love most about your family?

_____
_____
_____
_____
_____

What can you do to be a light in your home?

_____
_____
_____
_____

Day 36: Daily Journal

DAY 37: Optimistic

Today's Confession
Read Aloud

I decree and declare that I am optimistic and positive. My perspective is based on heaven's purpose. My steps are in order with God's plan for my life. My words come into divine alignment with God's Word.

Day 37: What It Means to Be and What Is

- Optimism: A tendency to expect the best possible outcome, dwell on the most hopeful outcome, or dwell on the most hopeful aspects of a situation.[66]

- Positive: 3. Admitting of no doubt; irrefutable. 4. Very sure; confident.[67]

Day 37: Bread for the Soul

Romans 8:28 And we know that all things work together for good to them that love God, to them who are called according to his purpose (KJV).

Philippians 4:8 Finally, brothers, whatever is true, whatever is noble, whatever is right, whatever is pure, whatever is lovely, whatever is admirable—if anything is excellent or praiseworthy—think about such things (NIV).

Day 37: Today's Prayer
Read Aloud

Christ Jesus, I pray that You will change my outlook on life. Lord let my perception change to Your perception. God, I know that no matter what happens, You have a plan. Christ Jesus, You have given me the grace to see Your light in the darkness. I pray that every negative mind-set over my life will be broken in Jesus' Name. Holy Spirit, please break any negative perception I may have of myself. Christ Jesus, please break every stronghold now. Through the blood of Jesus, I command the kingdom of darkness to loosen its hold over my mind. Holy Spirit, free my mental process. I decree and declare that I will always lift my hands to worship Christ Jesus. I will always find a reason to worship You, Lord; You know the beginning to the end. God you are good. In Christ Jesus' Name I pray. Amen.

Day 37: Be Encouraged

Life is rooted in perception. No matter what happens in a day, the way a situation affects us all depends on how we perceive it. God wants you to have a positive outlook on life. He is aware of the pressures that young people continually face. Being positive and having other good character traits come with practice. Positive people spend less time sitting around pondering situations and instead get up and act. Being positive is part of having faith.

Day 37: Today's Goal

For the next three days, choose to see the good in every situation around you. No matter what it looks like, find something in it to give, God thanks.

Day 37: From Your Own Perspective

When unplanned things happen, is it a moment to dwell in disappointment or look for a positive escape in your mind?

_____
_____
_____

What situation in your own life can you choose to change your perspective on today?

_____
_____
_____
_____

Day 37: Daily Journal

DAY 38: Well Done

Today's Confession
Read Aloud

I decree and declare that I have a purpose and destiny in the Kingdom of the Living God and on earth. I will successfully walk in them. At the end of all things, God will say to me, "Well done."

Day 38: What It Means to Be and What Is

- Purpose: 1. An aim or goal. 2. A result or effect that is intended or desired; intention.[68]

- Destiny: A predetermined course of events.[69]

Day 38: Bread for the Soul

Jeremiah 1:4–5 The word of the Lord came to me saying, "Before I formed you in the womb I knew you, before you were born I set you apart"(NIV).

Ephesians 1:3–11 Blessed be the God and Father of our Lord Jesus Christ, who hath blessed us with all spiritual blessings in heavenly places in Christ: According as he hath chosen us in him before the foundation of the world, that we should be holy and without blame before him in love. Having predestinated us unto the adoption of children by Jesus Christ to himself, according to the pleasure of his will. To the praise of the glory of his grace, wherein he hath made us acceptable in the beloved. In whom we have redemption through his blood, for the forgiveness of sins, according to the riches of his grace; Wherein he hath abounded toward us in all wisdom and prudence; having made known unto us the mystery of his will, according to his good pleasure which he hath purposed in himself. That in the dispensation of the fullness of times he might gather together in one all things in Christ, both which are in heaven, and which are on earth, even in him: in whom we have obtained an inheritance, being predestined according to the purpose of him who worketh all things after the counsel of his own will (KJV).

2 Timothy 4:7-8 I have fought the good fight, I have finished the race, I have kept the faith. Now there is in store for me the crown of righteousness, which the Lord, the righteous Judge, will award to me on that day; and not only to me, but also to all who have longed for his appearing (NIV).

Romans 8:28 For those God foreknew he also predestined to be conformed to the likeness of his Son, that he might be the firstborn among many brothers. And those he predestined, he also called; those he called, he also justified; those he justified, he also glorified (NIV).

Day 38: Today's Prayer
Read Aloud

Christ Jesus, I thank You for Your love. Thank You, Lord, for accepting me in the beloved. Lord, I just pray that You will continue to bring forth the promises You have placed upon my life. Lord, I decree and declare that You are restoring all things. I give heaven notice this day that I am ready to step into my divine destiny. Call out to my soul, God of Israel, and let the sound bring me closer to You. Lord, through the blood of Jesus Christ, tear down every negative word spoken over my destiny and life. Those negative things will not come to pass in my life, in Jesus' Name. I believe Your Word, Father, when it says greater is He who is within me than he who is in the world **(1 John 4:4)**. No matter what people say about me, I know Christ Jesus has the final say. In Christ Jesus' Name I pray. Amen.

Day 38: Be Encouraged

You are *never* too young to start walking in your destiny. David was still a boy when he was anointed king of Israel, even though his kingship happened later in his life. He was a king the moment God spoke it into existence.

(1 Samuel 16:1–13). You are who God says you are the moment He speaks it into existence regardless of whether you can physically see it yet. David was a boy when he had victory over the giant Goliath **(1 Samuel 17)**. The prophet Jeremiah was young when God called him to speak to the nations **(Jeremiah 1:1–9)**. Jesus started teaching in the synagogues when He was just a boy **(Luke 1:41–52)**. Today is your day. Make a choice to step into your destiny, and take the world by storm.

Day 38: Today's Goal

Read the story of Jeremiah today. (Jeremiah 1:1–9) What can you take from it?

Day 38: From Your Own Perspective

Who do you believe you are to God? After you have sought the answer from Him, what did He reveal?

_____
_____
_____
_____

God has kept you, and it was for a reason. How will you thank God for His grace in your life?

_____
_____
_____
_____

What will you do with the time and grace God has given you?

_____
_____

Day 38: Daily Journal

DAY 39: Something New

Today's Confession
Read Aloud

I decree and declare that today is a new day; the past is over, and I am made new. I am marked by the mouth of God. God calls me His own.

Day 39: Bread for the Soul

Isaiah 43:18-19 Forget the former things; do not dwell on the past. See I am doing a new thing! Now it springs up; do you not perceive it? I am making a way in the desert and streams in the wasteland (NIV).

Genesis 41:51 Joseph named his firstborn Manasseh and said, "It is because God has made me to forget all my trouble" (NIV).

1 Chronicles 22:9 But you will have a son who will be a man of peace and rest, and I will give him rest from all his enemies on every side. His name will be Solomon, and I will grant Israel peace and quiet during his reign (NIV).

Psalm 44:26 Rise up and help us; redeem us because of your unfailing love (NIV).

Psalm 51:1–2, 7 Have mercy on me, O God, according to your unfailing love; according to your great compassion blot out all my transgressions. Cleanse me with hyssop and I will be clean; wash me and I will be whiter than snow (NIV).

Psalm 62:1–2 My soul finds rest in God alone; my salvation comes from Him. He alone is my rock and my salvation; he is my fortress, I will never be shaken (NIV).

Psalm 121:1–2 I lift up my eyes to the hills—where does my help come from? My help comes from the Lord, the Maker of heaven and earth (NIV).

Also see the following:
Psalm 119:145–146, 149, 154, 156

Isaiah 26:7–10

Day 39: Today's Prayer
Read Aloud

Christ Jesus, I give You the glory for all You have done in my life. I thank You, Lord, for erasing my past. Lord, I pray that as You did for Joseph, You will make me forget all pain. (**Genesis 41:51**) Christ Jesus, I pray that as You did for Solomon, You will give me rest from all my enemies on every side. (**1 Kings 5:4**) Lord, I pray that the residue of the past be removed from my spirit. Lord, please grant me the stability and security that is in You. Create in me a pure heart, O God, and renew a steadfast spirit within me. Do not cast me from Your presence or take Your Holy Spirit from me. Restore to me the joy of Your Salvation, and grant me a willing Spirit to sustain me. (**Psalm 51:10-12**) Rise up and help me; redeem me because of Your unfailing love. (**Psalm 44:26**) Have mercy upon me, O God, according to Your unfailing love; according to Your great compassion, blot out my transgressions. Wash away all my iniquity and cleanse me from my sin. Cleanse me with hyssop and I will be clean; wash me and I will be whiter than snow. **(Psalm 51:1-2, 7)** Save me, O God, by Your name; vindicate me by Your might. Hear my prayer, O God; listen to the words of my mouth. **(Psalm 53:2)** My soul finds rest in God alone; my salvation comes from Him. He alone is my rock and my salvation; He is my fortress, and I will never be shaken. **(Psalms 62:5-6)** I call with all my heart; answer me, O Lord, and I will obey Your decrees. I call out to You; save me, and I will keep Your statues. **(Psalms 119: 145-146)** Hear my voice in accordance with Your love; preserve my life, O Lord, according to Your laws. **(Psalms 119: 149)** Defend my cause and redeem me; preserve my life according to Your promise. **(Psalms 119:154)** My help comes from the Lord, the maker of heaven and earth. **(Psalms 121:2)** Your compassion is great, O Lord. **(Psalms 119:156)** The path of the righteous is level; O upright One, You make the way of the righteous smooth. Yes, Lord, walking in the way of Your laws, I wait for You; Your Name and renown are the desires of my heart. My soul yearns for You in the night; in the morning my spirit longs for You. **(Isaiah 26:7-9)** May the morning bring me word of Your unfailing love. **(Psalms 143:8)** Vindicate me, God. **(Psalms 43:1)** In Christ Jesus' Name I pray. Amen.

Day 39: Be Encouraged

Sometimes we human beings spend too much thinking on what has been, rather than looking ahead. Often we are stuck looking at the mural of our past, while God is trying to get our attention to the masterpiece He has created of our future. No person on this earth has made all of the right decisions, but those who recover from their mistakes are the ones who decide to move forward. The kingdom of God itself is always advancing; the glory of God is never ending.

God wants you to simply drop the weight of your past today. Stop carrying it around; it is dead weight. Don't get caught in the trap of believing, "I know this is what God thinks of me". Who knows the mind of God? He said in His word that His thoughts toward you are of good and not of evil. (Jeremiah 29:11) No matter what your past is, Christ Jesus will never, ever turn you away. Today is a new day. Pick up that paintbrush called faith, and paint the mural that reflects the newness God is birthing in you. Be blessed.

John 6:35 and 37 Then Jesus declared…"All that the Father gives me will come to me, and whoever comes to me I will never drive away."

Day 39: From Your Own Perspective

What things in your past do you need to let go of?

_____
_____
_____
_____
_____

Have you allowed God to give you peace over the past?

_____
_____
_____
_____
_____

Day 39: Daily Journal

DAY 40: And it Was So

Today's Confession
Read Aloud

Whenever life seems tough...when I have the questions but not all the answers...whenever temptation comes—I will stand on the Word of God and decree and declare that, "I am."
I belong to the I AM WHO I AM.

Day 40: Bread for Your Soul

Exodus 3:13–15 Moses said to God, "Suppose I go to the Israelites and say to them, 'The God of your fathers has sent me to you,' and they ask me, 'What is his name?' Then what shall I tell them?" God said Moses, "I AM WHO I AM. This is what you are to say to the Israelites: 'I AM has sent me to you.'"

John 8:58 "I tell you the truth," Jesus answered, "before Abraham was, I am!"

Day 40: Today's Prayer
Read Aloud

Lord, I thank You for the work You have done in my life. Thank You for allowing me to know more of You. Christ Jesus, this is just the beginning. I pray that You will continue to speak to me. Give me the words, Lord; speak to my spirit. I want to know what You would have me confess over myself. Lord, let a guard be over my mouth so that I won't say anything that will negatively affect my future. I thank You, Lord, simply because You are God. Lord, on this journey of life, let my hand always be in Your hand. You are beautiful, and Your wonders echo throughout the ages. In the Name that is above every name, in the matchless Name of my Lord and Savior Jesus Christ I pray. Amen.

Day 40: Be Encouraged

I hope this book has helped you and encouraged your soul. You have the opportunity to continue to use these confessions to your advantage. You can pick your favorite one or multiple ones if you want to do that. Go through this book as many times as you like. If you are ever at a loss for words, the prayers in this book are there to help. Continue to welcome God in and watch your life take heaven's form. **May the Lord bless you and keep you; the Lord make his face shine upon you and be gracious to you; the Lord turn his face toward you and give you peace (NIV). Numbers 6:24-26**

Day 40: Today's Goal

There is a section in this book where you can write out your own confessions. What do you want to be in the future? What are your goals? Where do you want to travel? What type of success do you want to see in your tomorrow? Do you want to be a doctor, lawyer, chef, musician or veterinarian? Do you want your own family some day? In what way do you want to experience God? Write it down; confess it over yourself daily. Give notice to the earthly realm where you are headed. Give heaven notice that you are in need of help and guidance to accomplish those things. Remember, Christ Jesus loves you, and that will never change. No matter what happens, remember Whose you are. You serve the I AM WHO I AM. Remember you are a star. A rare gem in the hand of God. So shine bright!

Day 40: From Your Own Perspective

What have you gained from reading this book?
_____
_____
_____
_____

What positive changes have you made in your life?
_____
_____
_____
_____
_____

Has this book helped you to influence another person's life?
_____
_____
_____
_____
_____

Will you choose to operate in divine power from this day forward? Will your words reflect what God has said about you? Will you stand and fight!

Day 40: Daily Journal

Create Your Own Confessions

(_____) Daily Confessions
Insert Your Name

School Day Ready!

This is a great way to start the day! Here is a list of confessions you can proclaim over yourself every morning before school. It takes less than 3 minutes, but sets the tone for the rest of your day.

1. Today is a new day!
2. Christ Jesus loves me
3. I am a leader
4. I am powerful
5. I am confident
6. I am successful
7. I am a world changer
8. I have the favor of God
9. I am happy
10. No weapon formed against me shall prosper. I plead Psalms 91, Psalms 23, and the blood of Jesus over myself. In Christ Jesus' Name, it is so. Amen.

List of Daily Confessions

Here is a complete list of the confessions you have proclaimed over yourself during this journey. Use them anytime. May God continually bless and keep you.

1. I exercise my divine right on the earth this day to speak change into my present and future. I will decree a thing, and it will be established. I will declare a thing, and it shall come to pass.

2. I decree and declare that I am attentive and alert to the movements of heaven. I open my soul to the frequencies of the throne room of the Eternal God. I will have a divine encounter with Christ Jesus.

3. I decree and declare that I love Christ Jesus with all my heart, my mind, my strength, and all that I am. I know and accept that Christ Jesus loves me unconditionally and forever.

4. I decree and declare that I am obedient, cooperative, and respectful.

5. I decree and declare that I am a powerful and effective leader. My leadership skills will open divine doors for me.

6. I decree and declare that I am smart, spiritually intelligent, and an academic genius. I excel in all my studies. I carry wisdom of the kingdom of God inside me.

7. I decree and declare that through the blood and salvation of Christ Jesus, I am powerful beyond the measure of the sands on the seashore. I will exercise that power within the will of Christ Jesus. I am armed and ready for battle through the Spirit of the Living God.

8. (For Young Men). I decree and declare that I am handsome, chivalrous, a mighty man of valor, noble, chaste, a warrior before the Lord, and a prince in the kingdom of the Living God.

(For Young Ladies). I decree and declare that I am absolutely gorgeous and beautiful inside and out. I am clothed in strength and dignity. I am virtuous. I decree and declare that I am elegant, noble, worth far more than rubies, a treasure, a young lady who fears the Lord, and a princess in the kingdom of the Living God.

9. I decree and declare that I love and accept myself. I accept who Christ Jesus says I am. From this day forward, I will see myself only as God sees me. I am a holy nation, the head and not the tail, a friend of God, the lender and not the borrower.

10. I decree and declare that the favor of God rests upon my life. I am loved and celebrated by all who come in contact with me.

11. I decree and declare that I am lionhearted and as innocent as a dove.

12. I decree and declare that I will practice an attitude of gratitude. I am always appreciative and thankful.

13. I decree and declare that I make friends easily. I am confident and outgoing. I am a fun, friendly, and wise person. I am a positive influence on those around me.

14. I decree and declare that I am humble in spirit, my attitude, and my actions. I will seek to exalt Christ Jesus at all times.

15. I decree and declare that I am walking in divine rulership granted by the Living God. Christ Jesus has granted me citizenship in the kingdom of the Eternal God.

16. I decree and declare that I practice justice with all those around me. I am forgiving, merciful, and gracious.

17. I decree and declare that I am always improving, both in my walk with Christ Jesus and in the natural realm. I am always getting better. My spirit will flourish in the Kingdom of the Living God.

18. I decree and declare that I will endure in the ways of Christ Jesus until the end. I will never give up. I will never quit. I am a champion.

19. I decree and declare that I am trustworthy, honest, and a person of integrity.

20. I decree and declare that I am happy and joyful. I always have a reason to smile. I have the peace of God, that surpasses all understanding.

21. I decree and declare that I am whole. No good thing is lacking in my life.

22. I decree and declare that I am faithful and diligent. I practice self-discipline in positive and righteous ways.

23. I decree and declare that I am prosperous and opulent. I am spiritually prosperous in Christ Jesus.

24. I decree and declare that I live in perfect physical, emotional, and mental health. I decree and declare that by

Jesus stripes I am healed. I have spiritual health through the blood of Christ Jesus and the Word of God.

25. I decree and declare that my creative power through Christ Jesus takes me to places beyond earthly creation. The transformation of my world starts with a change of mind.

26. I decree and declare that my soul is a divine carrier of God's glory. The Lord is a wall of fire around me. Christ Jesus is my glory within. I am the very beat of God's heart. I am the apple of God's eye.

27. I decree and declare that I will eternally walk in love. My heart is an ocean where God can pour in so that I may pour into others. My well will never run dry.

28. I decree and declare that I am generous, thoughtful, and one who sows into others.

29. I decree and declare that I am saved and have received salvation through Jesus Christ's blood. I am a citizen of the Kingdom of God. I am forgiven.

30. I decree and declare that the Holy Spirit guides me and lives inside of me. My ears are open to hear what He is saying. Rivers of living water will flow from within me.

31. I decree and declare that I am free. I am free from every stronghold of the enemy. I am free from everything that opposes the divine nature God has placed within me.

32. I decree and declare that I am spiritually, mentally, and physically safe through the blood of Christ Jesus. No weapon formed against me shall prosper.

33. I decree and declare that I trust God with my very life and all that I am. I will never withhold any part of myself from Christ Jesus.

34. I decree and declare that I am a world changer. I am a general in the kingdom of God. I know that heaven will remember my name. My life will be a divine testimony that eternity will never forget.

35. I decree and declare that I have great zeal for the Lord. My soul is on fire for the Eternal God. I am one who worships God in spirit and in truth.

36. I decree and declare that Christ Jesus is the Lord and Head of my family. I am loyal and thankful for those God has given me as family. My family is growing in unity every day.

37. I decree and declare that I am optimistic and positive. My perspective is based on heaven's purpose. My steps are in order with God's plan for my life. My words come into divine alignment with God's Word.

38. I decree and declare that I have a purpose and destiny in the kingdom of the living God and on earth. I will successfully walk in them. At the end of all things, God will say to me, "Well done."

39. I decree and declare that today is a new day; the past is over, and I am made new. I am marked by the mouth of God. God calls me His own.

40. Whenever life seems tough…when I have the questions but not all the answers…whenever temptation comes—I will stand on the Word of God and decree and declare that, "I am." I belong to the I AM WHO I AM.

Your Words Have Power!

Notes

Preface

[1] *The American Heritage Dictionary, Fourth Edition* (New York: Houghton Mifflin Company, 2001), "spell"

[2] *The American Heritage Dictionary, Fourth Edition* (New York: Houghton Mifflin Company, 2001), "snare"

[3] *The American Heritage Dictionary, Fourth Edition* (New York: Houghton Mifflin Company, 2001), "stronghold"

Day 1

[4] *The American Heritage Dictionary, Fourth Edition* (New York: Houghton Mifflin Company, 2001), "Divine"

[5] *The American Heritage Dictionary, Fourth Edition* (New York: Houghton Mifflin Company, 2001), "Right"

[6] *The American Heritage Dictionary, Fourth Edition* (New York: Houghton Mifflin Company, 2001), "Decree"

[7] *The American Heritage Dictionary, Fourth Edition* (New York: Houghton Mifflin Company, 2001), "Declare"

[8] *The American Heritage Dictionary, Fourth Edition* (New York: Houghton Mifflin Company, 2001), "Likeness"

[9] *The American Heritage Dictionary, Fourth Edition* (New York: Houghton Mifflin Company, 2001), "Image"

Day 3

[10] *The American Heritage Dictionary, Fourth Edition* (New York: Houghton Mifflin Company, 2001), "Heart"

Day 4

[11] *The American Heritage Dictionary, Fourth Edition* (New York: Houghton Mifflin Company, 2001), "Obedient"

[12] *The American Heritage Dictionary, Fourth Edition* (New York: Houghton Mifflin Company, 2001), "Cooperate"

[13] *The American Heritage Dictionary, Fourth Edition* (New York: Houghton Mifflin Company, 2001), "Cooperative"

[14] *The American Heritage Dictionary, Fourth Edition* (New York: Houghton Mifflin Company, 2001), "Respect"

Day 5

[15] *The American Heritage Dictionary, Fourth Edition* (New York: Houghton Mifflin Company, 2001), "Lead"

[16] *The American Heritage Dictionary, Fourth Edition* (New York: Houghton Mifflin Company, 2001), "Effect"

Day 6

[17] *The American Heritage Dictionary, Fourth Edition* (New York: Houghton Mifflin Company, 2001), "Smart"

[18] *The American Heritage Dictionary, Fourth Edition* (New York: Houghton Mifflin Company, 2001), "Intelligent"

[19] *The American Heritage Dictionary, Fourth Edition* (New York: Houghton Mifflin Company, 2001), "Genius"

[20] *The American Heritage Dictionary, Fourth Edition* (New York: Houghton Mifflin Company, 2001), "DNA"

Day 7

[21] *The American Heritage Dictionary, Fourth Edition* (New York: Houghton Mifflin Company, 2001), "Power"

[22] *The American Heritage Dictionary, Fourth Edition* (New York: Houghton Mifflin Company, 2001), "Measure"

Day 8

[23] *The American Heritage Dictionary, Fourth Edition* (New York: Houghton Mifflin Company, 2001), "Handsome"

[24] *The American Heritage Dictionary, Fourth Edition* (New York: Houghton Mifflin Company, 2001), "Chivalry"

[25] *The American Heritage Dictionary, Fourth Edition* (New York: Houghton Mifflin Company, 2001), "Mighty"

[26] *The American Heritage Dictionary, Fourth Edition* (New York: Houghton Mifflin Company, 2001), "Valor"

[27] *The American Heritage Dictionary, Fourth Edition* (New York: Houghton Mifflin Company, 2001), "Chaste"

[28] *The American Heritage Dictionary, Fourth Edition* (New York: Houghton Mifflin Company, 2001), "Nobility"

[29] *The American Heritage Dictionary, Fourth Edition* (New York: Houghton Mifflin Company, 2001), "Noble"

[30] *The American Heritage Dictionary, Fourth Edition* (New York: Houghton Mifflin Company, 2001), "Warrior"

[31] *The American Heritage Dictionary, Fourth Edition* (New York: Houghton Mifflin Company, 2001), "Prince"

[32] *The American Heritage Dictionary, Fourth Edition* (New York: Houghton Mifflin Company, 2001), "Gorgeous"

[33] *The American Heritage Dictionary, Fourth Edition* (New York: Houghton Mifflin Company, 2001), "Beauty"

[34] *The American Heritage Dictionary, Fourth Edition* (New York: Houghton Mifflin Company, 2001), "Virtue"

[35] *The American Heritage Dictionary, Fourth Edition* (New York: Houghton Mifflin Company, 2001), "Elegance"

[36] *The American Heritage Dictionary, Fourth Edition* (New York: Houghton Mifflin Company, 2001), "Nobility"

[37] *The American Heritage Dictionary, Fourth Edition* (New York: Houghton Mifflin Company, 2001), "Noble"

[38] *The American Heritage Dictionary, Fourth Edition* (New York: Houghton Mifflin Company, 2001), "Treasure"

[39] *The American Heritage Dictionary, Fourth Edition* (New York: Houghton Mifflin Company, 2001), "Princess"

Day 10

[40] *The American Heritage Dictionary, Fourth Edition* (New York: Houghton Mifflin Company, 2001), "Favor"

Day 11

[41] *The American Heritage Dictionary, Fourth Edition* (New York: Houghton Mifflin Company, 2001), "Lionhearted"

[42] *The American Heritage Dictionary, Fourth Edition* (New York: Houghton Mifflin Company, 2001), "Innocent"

Day 12

[43] *The American Heritage Dictionary, Fourth Edition* (New York: Houghton Mifflin Company, 2001), "Appreciate"

Day 13

[44] *The American Heritage Dictionary, Fourth Edition* (New York: Houghton Mifflin Company, 2001), "Friend"

[45] *The American Heritage Dictionary, Fourth Edition* (New York: Houghton Mifflin Company, 2001), "Friendly"

Day 14

[46] *The American Heritage Dictionary, Fourth Edition* (New York: Houghton Mifflin Company, 2001), "Humble"

Day 15

[47] *The American Heritage Dictionary, Fourth Edition* (New York: Houghton Mifflin Company, 2001), "Ruler"

[48] *The American Heritage Dictionary, Fourth Edition* (New York: Houghton Mifflin Company, 2001), "Ruling"

Day 16

[49] *The American Heritage Dictionary, Fourth Edition* (New York: Houghton Mifflin Company, 2001), "Justice"

[50] *The American Heritage Dictionary, Fourth Edition* (New York: Houghton Mifflin Company, 2001), "Forgive"

51 *The American Heritage Dictionary, Fourth Edition* (New York: Houghton Mifflin Company, 2001), "Mercy"

52 *The American Heritage Dictionary, Fourth Edition* (New York: Houghton Mifflin Company, 2001), "Gracious"

Day 18

53 *The American Heritage Dictionary, Fourth Edition* (New York: Houghton Mifflin Company, 2001), "Endure"

54 *The American Heritage Dictionary, Fourth Edition* (New York: Houghton Mifflin Company, 2001), "Champion"

Day 19

55 *The American Heritage Dictionary, Fourth Edition* (New York: Houghton Mifflin Company, 2001), "Trustworthy"

56 *The American Heritage Dictionary, Fourth Edition* (New York: Houghton Mifflin Company, 2001), "Honest"

57 *The American Heritage Dictionary, Fourth Edition* (New York: Houghton Mifflin Company, 2001), "Integrity"

Day 22

58 *The American Heritage Dictionary, Fourth Edition* (New York: Houghton Mifflin Company, 2001), "Faithful"

59 *The American Heritage Dictionary, Fourth Edition* (New York: Houghton Mifflin Company, 2001), "Diligent"

60 *The American Heritage Dictionary, Fourth Edition* (New York: Houghton Mifflin Company, 2001), "Discipline"

Day 23

[61] *The American Heritage Dictionary, Fourth Edition* (New York: Houghton Mifflin Company, 2001), "Prosperous"

[62] *The American Heritage Dictionary, Fourth Edition* (New York: Houghton Mifflin Company, 2001), "Opulent"

Day 25

[63] *The American Heritage Dictionary, Fourth Edition* (New York: Houghton Mifflin Company, 2001), "Imagination"

Day 28

[64] *The American Heritage Dictionary, Fourth Edition* (New York: Houghton Mifflin Company, 2001), "Generous"

[65] *The American Heritage Dictionary, Fourth Edition* (New York: Houghton Mifflin Company, 2001), "Thoughtful"

Day 37

[66] *The American Heritage Dictionary, Fourth Edition* (New York: Houghton Mifflin Company, 2001), "Optimism"

[67] *The American Heritage Dictionary, Fourth Edition* (New York: Houghton Mifflin Company, 2001), "Positive"

Day 38

[68] *The American Heritage Dictionary, Fourth Edition* (New York: Houghton Mifflin Company, 2001), "Purpose"

[69] *The American Heritage Dictionary, Fourth Edition* (New York: Houghton Mifflin Company, 2001), "Positive"

www.ingramcontent.com/pod-product-compliance
Lightning Source LLC
Chambersburg PA
CBHW071900290426
44110CB00013B/1217